GOD'S KINGDOM FOR TODAY

PETER TOON

WIPF & STOCK · Eugene, Oregon

Wipf and Stock Publishers
199 W 8th Ave, Suite 3
Eugene, OR 97401

God's Kingdom For Today
By Toon, Peter
Copyright©1980 by Toon, Peter
ISBN 13: 978-1-5326-4404-7
Publication date 11/21/2017
Previously published by Cornerstone Books, 1980

CONTENTS

PREFACE

The origin of this book lies in the study I did to prepare the lectures which I delivered to an audience representing many denonimations in St. Giles-in-the-Fields, London, in October and November 1979. The topic of the kingdom of God was suggested to me in 1978 by the Rector, the Rev. Gordon Taylor.

No reader of the Scriptures can doubt that the theme of the kingdom of God is prominent in its pages. It is especially prominent in the teaching of Jesus. Further, no student of the history of Christian thought can doubt that the theme of the kingdom has captivated the interest not only of great intellectuals, but also of many other people as well.

What I present here is my understanding of what the biblical teaching on the kingdom of God (= "kingdom of heaven") means and what is its relevance for today. I have not written for theologians or experts, but rather for the ordinary, committed Christian who wishes to explore this important theme with the help of a guide.

I dedicate this book to the Reverend Dr. John Stott, who in recent years has heartily encouraged Christians

to see the appropriate social and political commitment
involved in the privilege of being faithful disciples of the
kingdom.

I also thank Miss Christine Money for doing the basic
typing.

My quotations are mostly from the *Revised Standard
Version*. I have added discussion questions at the end of
each chapter in order to make the book useful for
church study groups.

Peter Toon
All Saints' Day
1st November 1979
Oak Hill College, London

PART I   EXPOSITION

1 THE OLD TESTAMENT

When you or I speak to a person, we adapt our speech to what we believe are the capacities of the person. Talking to a child, we normally use simple words and sentences. Talking to a brilliant intellectual, we may use difficult words and long sentences. In other words, we operate a principle of accommodation, accommodating ourselves to the capacities of our hearers. Whether we succeed or fail is not here in question. The point is that normally we use this principle even when we do it unconsciously.

Through the centuries, Christian teachers and theologians have spoken and written of God as accommodating himself to our capacities. God, who is infinite and eternal and thus beyond our reach, has revealed himself to human beings. He has disclosed himself to sinful people. He has spoken to finite humans in ways they can understand. He has addressed the average kind of person and spoken in such a way that that person can grasp what is being said.

This activity of God in speaking to mankind in an intelligible way is related to distinct actions by God in

human history and affairs. What we have in the Old
Testament is a record of God's activity, usually on behalf
of a particular people (Israel), along with God's own
words preparing for, explaining, and developing the
meaning of these acts of God. There is also, of course,
the response of the people to God's action and words
together with God's comments on this response.

What I am here affirming is the close connection within
God's self-disclosure and revelation of action and
explanatory word. God reveals himself in both act and
word, and certainly in word, for without explanations
events can have many possible interpretations. Further,
according to the principle of accommodation when God
speaks, he speaks in terms that can be understood by the
hearers, in their language and using their culture.

Against this background I can now state what it is that
I want to present in this chapter. First, I want to assert
that in revealing himself to the people of Israel, God
actually called himself the King *(melek)* and spoke of his
kingdom *(malkuth* and related nouns). Secondly, I want
also to assert that this picture of God is intimately associated with the experience of the LORD enjoyed by
the Israelites in their covenant relationship with him.
Thirdly, I want to explain what these images or pictures
of king and kingdom represented in terms of the Old
Testament view of God.

GOD AS KING

We begin at Mount Sinai. Following the experience of
deliverance from slavery and bondage in Egypt came
the experience of the overpowering, numinous, glorious, and almighty presence of the LORD on the mountain. The holy Presence was announced and symbolized
by earthquake, smoke, and wind; and God, the LORD,

entered into a covenant with these former slaves. He became their sovereign LORD, and they became his worshiping, obedient people. This was not an agreement between equals; it was an agreement of the almighty with the weak, the holy with the sinful, and the righteous with the unrighteous. The Israelites gained the Lord as their Guide, Protector, Leader, Savior, and Friend. He gained a disobedient people, but a people through whom he intended to speak to the whole world.

Tribes who had been slaves of the great king Pharaoh now became the servants of the great LORD, the God of Abraham, Isaac, and Jacob. In those days, kings of empires ruled as absolute monarchs and were worshiped as gods. At Sinai, the Israelites gained a new, absolute monarch, an almighty ruler, an invisible King, a King who is the Creator of the world. It surely made sense in terms of the understanding of kingship in the ancient Near East for God to begin to speak to the Israelites of himself as the King, as their King and the King of the world. For in many ways the LORD related to them as a great King—the God of authority, power, leadership, protection, and so on.

The idea of kingship of the LORD is suggested in various ways in the way God spoke to Israel in the experience of the Exodus and at the foot of Mount Sinai. For example, the LORD said, "Now therefore, if you will obey my voice and keep my covenant you shall be my own possession among all peoples; for all the earth is mine, and you shall be to me a kingdom of priests and a holy nation" (Exodus 19:5, 6). Here God, accommodating himself to the people, pictures himself as ruling over a people all of whom offer him true worship and loving obedience, which is the ideal of the covenant. Also there is the song of Moses, sung after the deliverance from

Egypt. In this he praised the LORD, their leader and deliverer, and ended with the words, "The LORD will reign for ever and ever" (Exodus 15:18). Here the servant of God, inspired by God, addresses the LORD as King.

At the center of the movable sanctuary which we know as the Tabernacle was the ark of the covenant. This "box" contained the tablets on which was written the Law, and it also functioned in an important way as the throne of the invisible King, the sign of his presence. Several times we read about "the ark of the covenant of the Lord of hosts who is enthroned on the cherubim" (1 Samuel 4:4; 2 Samuel 6:2; 2 Kings 19:15; etc.). The cherubim were creatures with large wings made of gold and attached to the top of the ark—that is, to the mercy seat. The Lord met Moses and spoke to him "above the mercy seat and between the two cherubim" (Exodus 25:22). Later in the history of Israel, when the ark was taken into the Temple of Jerusalem, the glory of the Lord filled the sanctuary (1 Kings 8:11), for God had descended to his throne.

Here, with the thought of the ark as the throne of the invisible King and of the LORD descending, as it were, to sit on the outstretched wings of the cherubim, we are in the realm of dynamic symbolism, the realm of controlled imagination and faith. The ark was the focal point which served to bring into the spiritual sight of the faithful Israelites a sense of the presence of the LORD and thoughts of him as the great King. In other words, the ark served both to evoke experience of God and to increase understanding of his relation to Israel.

In the worship of the Temple, especially at festivals, the kingship of the LORD was celebrated and proclaimed. The faithful Israelites believed that they actually experienced the saving power and rule of the LORD as they worshiped. They cried:

Make a joyful noise to the LORD, all the earth;
break forth into joyous song and sing praises!
With trumpets and the sound of the horn
make a joyful noise before the King,
the LORD!

(Psalm 98:4, 6)

And,

Sing praises to God, sing praises!
Sing praises to our King, sing praises!
For God is the king of all the earth;
sing praises with a psalm!

(Psalm 47:6, 7)

Although the LORD is proclaimed as the King over all, the ark remains the symbol of that rule:

The LORD reigns; let the peoples tremble!
He sits enthroned upon the cherubim;
let the earth quake!
The LORD is great in Zion,
he is exalted over all the peoples.

(Psalm 99:1, 2)

And,

God reigns over the nations;
God sits on his holy throne.

(Psalm 47:8)

A study of such Psalms as 47, 93, 96, 97, 98, and 99, all of which celebrate the LORD as King, reveals that the rule of God is seen as being over all peoples, all history, and all creation. It is a universal rule which is particularly known and recognized in Israel.

An important aspect of the rule of the LORD over Israel was his concern for justice and righteousness in the community life of his covenant people and in their relations with other people. This included intervening on behalf of the widows, orphans, poor, destitute, and sick, as well as judging the wicked. Psalm 146, a theme of which is "The LORD will reign for ever . . . ," states this just action of the LORD.

Happy is he whose help is the God of Jacob,
   whose hope is in the Lord his God,
who made heaven and earth,
   the sea, and all that is in them;
who keeps faith for ever;
   who executes justice for the oppressed;
   who gives food to the hungry,
The LORD sets the prisoners free;
   the LORD opens the eyes of the blind.
The LORD lifts up those who are bowed down;
   the LORD loves the righteous.
The LORD watches over the sojourners,
   he upholds the widow and the fatherless;
   but the ways of the wicked he brings to ruin.

The same concern with the needy is found in the Torah—see e.g., Deuteronomy 24:14-22. One part of this section reads as follows: "You shall not pervert justice due to the sojourner (alien) or to the fatherless, or take a widow's garment in pledge; but you shall remember that you were a slave in Egypt and the LORD your God redeemed you from there; therefore I command you to do this" (vv. 17, 18). Thus, God's great act of liberation for the needy was to be the model for the attitude toward the weak and helpless in Israel.

It was in the Temple, in the year that King Uzziah died, that Isaiah had his vision of the LORD as King.

His vision is an enlargement of the basic idea of the LORD ruling from his throne over the ark. After experiencing a tremendous sense of the purity and holiness of God, Isaiah felt himself to be a hopeless and helpless sinner and to God he said, "Woe is me! For I am lost; for I am a man of unclean lips; and I dwell in the midst of a people of unclean lips; for my eyes have seen the King, the LORD of hosts!" (Isaiah 6:5). And the LORD revealed himself as the King of grace and mercy. Also, Jeremiah, who saw the collapse of the kingdom of Judah and the removal of the leaders to exile in Babylon, did not lose his belief in the LORD as the universal King. He asserted that the LORD ruled the Egyptian and the Babylonian empires even though they did not recognize him in worship (Jeremiah 46:18, 19; 48:15; 51:57).

The use of the term "King" for God, either by God himself or the Israelites, was not meant to be a full description of God (for he is also called Shepherd, Judge, etc.) or a scientifically accurate description of God (for God is beyond our knowledge and understanding). To call God King is to utilize an image, or more technically a model. Because God is of necessity greater than any human person, no human word or phrase can ever adequately describe him or his character. However, in certain obvious ways (and here is the strength of this model) there is a correspondence or identity between the human king and God. As the oriental king exercised ultimate power, protection, care, sovereignty, and authority in his empire and as he required the full obedience and worship of his subject people, so the LORD exercises power and authority in the universe and requires the full obedience of his chosen people. Yet, in other ways there is no correspondence. The LORD does not have a consort or queen or heir to his throne, and he does not run the risk of being conquered by another foreign king. Further, the LORD is perfectly holy, righteous, and merciful; in him is no imperfection or weakness.

Speaking in everyday terms of the ancient Near East, the positive analogy in a picture such as God as King was so obvious that the user of the image did not have to worry about the term being misunderstood. Today it is not quite the same. Only to the extent that we recognize what kind of king ruled in the ancient world will we see the positive analogy. This is why one of the rules for understanding the Bible is that we must understand the text in terms of the original situation in which the words were uttered and written.

GOD'S KINGDOM

In discussing the idea of the kingdom of God, we have to bear in mind that the Hebrew words *malkuth, melukah,* and *mamlakah* can be translated "reign," "rule," "dominion," and "kingdom." In other words, a territory is not necessarily always implied. The idea of the present kingdom or rule or reign of the LORD is found particularly in the Psalms.

For *dominion* belongs to the LORD,
and he rules over the nations.
             (Psalm 22:28; Hebrew *melukah*)

The LORD has established his throne in the heavens
and his *kingdom* rules over all.
             (Psalm 103:19; Hebrew *malkuth*)

All thy works shall give thanks to thee, O LORD,
and all thy saints shall bless thee!
They shall speak of the glory of thy *kingdom,*

and tell of thy power,
to make known to the sons of men thy mighty deeds
and the glorious splendor of thy *kingdom*.
Thy kingdom is an everlasting *kingdom*,
and thy dominion endures throughout all generations.

(Psalm 145:11-13; Hebrew *malkuth*)

David said:

Blessed art thou, O LORD, the God of Israel our father,
    for ever and ever.
Thine, O LORD, is the greatness, and the victory,
    and the majesty;
for all that is in the heavens and in the earth is thine;
thine is the *kingdom*, O LORD, and thou art exalted
    as head above all.
Both riches and honour come from thee,
and thou rulest over all.
In thy hands are power and might; and in thy hand it is
    to make great and to give strength to all.

(1 Chronicles 29:10-12; Hebrew *mamlakah*)

Here the kingdom of God is seen as the sovereign rule of the world by the LORD. He is in complete control of everything. However, his rule is particularly exhibited in his mighty acts on behalf of Israel—for example, in the deliverance from Egypt. In these Psalms there is no specific reference to the future when God the LORD will not only rule, but will be acknowledged by all to be ruling. For this teaching concerning the future, we must turn to the prophets.

The kingdom of the LORD will be established in the sense that the whole creation, cleansed of sin and imperfection, will perfectly respond to the LORD. As God had already acted decisively in redemption and judgment on behalf of his covenant people, so he will act again in a final and universal way. This will be the last of his "en-

trances" into human history and will close history to
bring into being a new order of reality. Amos spoke of
this intervention by God as a great time of judgment.
His contemporaries thought of God's coming only in
terms of rewards for themselves, and so Amos had to
tell them:

Woe to you who desire the day of the LORD!
   Why would you have the day of the LORD?
It is darkness and not light;
   as if a man fled from a lion,
   and a bear met him;
or went into the house and leaned
   with his hand against the wall,
   and a serpent bit him.
Is not the day of the LORD darkness,
   and not light,
   and gloom with no brightness in it?

                                        (Amos 5:18-20)

   Similar themes of judgment may be found in other
prophets. We shall return to this topic in Chapter Eight.
   The theme of the kingdom of God is presented by
Isaiah in terms of the total renewal of the universe and a
restored Jerusalem.

   For behold, I create
new heavens and a new earth.
   Former things shall no more be remembered
   nor shall they be called to mind.
   Rejoice and be filled with delight,
   you boundless realms which I create;
for I create Jerusalem to be a delight
   and her people a joy;
I will take delight in Jerusalem and rejoice in my people;
   weeping and cries for help
   shall never again be heard in her.

                                        (65:17-19, NEB)

These pictures are not to be taken literally, but they do clearly witness to the hope of a new order of reality which God himself will cause to come into being. Obadiah ends on this positive note: "And the Kingdom *(melukah)* shall be the LORD'S" (v. 21).

The themes of God the universal King and the final triumph of his kingdom (Hebrew *makelu*) at the end of the age are united in the contents of the book of Daniel. In his interpretation of Nebuchadnezzar's dream of the great image—having a head of gold, thighs of bronze, legs of iron, and feet of iron and clay; shattered by the great stone from the mountain—Daniel had the following to say: "The God of heaven will set up a kingdom which shall never be destroyed. . . . It shall break in pieces all these kingdoms [i.e., great empires of Daniel's day] and bring them to an end, and it shall stand for ever" (2:44). A little later in the book, Nebuchadnezzar is portrayed as celebrating the rule of God:

How great are his signs,
  how mighty his wonders!
His kingdom is an everlasting kingdom,
  and his dominion is from generation to generation.

(4:3)

Then in Chapter Seven the kingdom of the Messiah, the heavenly "Son of Man," is introduced as being integrally related to the eternal kingdom of God. This kingdom is given to the Messiah by God himself. In the Gospels we learn that Jesus made "Son of Man" the basic title by which he described himself, and in so doing he reflected his understanding of the prophecies in Daniel 7:13ff.

Having briefly presented the themes of the kingship and kingdom of God, we must look at two topics closely connected with these.

The kingdom of David and the kingdom of God

The conviction that the LORD ruled Israel was so strong that Gideon, the "judge," could declare, "I will not rule over you, neither shall my son rule you; but the Lord shall rule over you" (Judges 8:23). Later Samuel became angry when the people wanted to imitate the local nations and have a king to rule over them. On one occasion he told them, "But you have this day rejected your God, who saves you from all your calamities and your distresses and you have said, 'No! but set a king over us' " (1 Samuel 10:19).

In order to understand the relation of the kingdom of David to that of God, we must take note of the prophecy of Nathan addressed to David (2 Samuel 7:1-16). In this prophecy concerning the building of the Temple and the permanence of the Davidic line of kings are these words: "When your days are fulfilled and you lie down with your fathers, I will raise up your offspring after you, who shall come forth from your body and I will establish his kingdom. He shall build a house for my name and I will establish the throne of his kingdom for ever. I will be his father and he shall be my son. . . ." This idea of the king being the son of the LORD is expressed very powerfully in Psalm 2.

Based on this promise of the LORD to David, the throne of David and his successors can later be intimately related to the kingdom of the LORD himself. This is certainly what we find in the books of Chronicles. King David declared that the LORD "has chosen Solomon my son to sit upon the throne of the kingdom of the LORD over Israel" (1 Chronicles 28:5). Later Solomon is described as sitting "on the throne of the LORD as king instead of his father" (29:23). The Queen of Sheba addressed Solomon saying, "Blessed be the

LORD your God who has delighted in you and set you on his throne as king for the LORD your God" (2 Chronicles 9:8). Finally we note that Abijah, king of Judah, opposed Jeroboam, king of Israel, saying to him, "And now you think to withstand the kingdom of the LORD in the hands of the sons of David . . ." (13:8). This identification of the rule of the chosen king *and* of the LORD is a statement of what ought to have been the case and what to some extent was realized under certain kings. The rule of the Davidic kings should have ensured the faithful obedience and worship of the LORD by the people in their kingdom, so that they functioned as a "kingdom of priests" (Exodus 19:6). Regrettably, as the Old Testament makes clear, there was more failure than success. The kings did not ensure the rule of the LORD over their people. The Davidic kingdom was meant to be a kind of microcosm or symbol of the kingdom of God. It was to be a means of helping the people to understand what in fact was the kingdom of God.

The kingdom of the Messiah and the kingdom of God

Knowing the failure of the Davidic kings to rule in righteousness, the prophets, inspired by God, looked forward to a time within history and before the end of the age when a descendant of David would actually rule in justice, righteousness, and peace, eliminating all injustice and evil. Here are some passages from the prophecies of Isaiah:

For to us a child is born,
to us a son is given;
and the government will be upon his shoulder
and his name will be called
"Wonderful Counsellor, Mighty God,
Everlasting Father, Prince of Peace."

Of the increase of his government and peace
there will be no end,
upon the throne of David, and over his kingdom,
to establish it and to uphold it
with justice and with righteousness
from this time forth and for evermore.
The zeal of the LORD of hosts will do this.

(9:6, 7)

There shall come forth a shoot from the stem of Jesse,
and a branch shall grow out of his roots.
And the Spirit of the LORD shall rest upon him,
the spirit of wisdom and understanding,
the spirit of counsel and might,
the spirit of knowledge and the fear of the LORD,
and his delight shall be in the fear of the LORD.

(11:1-3)

Jesse was the father of David, and so the first two lines
of the second quotation are a poetic way of describing a
descendant of David. Jeremiah prophesied, "Behold,
the days are coming, says the LORD, when I will raise
up for David a righteous Branch and he shall reign as
king and deal wisely, and shall execute justice and righteousness in the land. In his days Judah will be saved,
and Israel will dwell securely. And this is the name by
which he will be called: 'The LORD is our righteousness' " (Jeremiah 23:5, 6).

This messianic kingdom has been interpreted in various ways by Christians. Some have believed, and do believe, on the basis of Revelation 20, that before the end
of history there will be a period, usually called the millennium, when Christ, the Messiah, will reign on earth
with or through his saints for 1,000 years. This is seen as
the culmination of his work as Lord and Savior and the
demonstration of his universal kingship.

Others believe that the total work of the Messiah from the beginning of his ministry in Galilee and including his present reign at the right hand of the Father (Acts 2:33) up to his return in glory to earth when his kingdom is handed over to the Father (1 Corinthians 15:24) is to be seen as the messianic kingdom. In this way of understanding the prophecies of the Old Testament, the symbolic rather than the literal sense is taken. Also, the millennium of Revelation 20 is taken symbolically. (My own view is that this way of looking at the matter is the better one, and I believe it to be confirmed by the way in which the apostles understood the fulfillment of prophecy as revealed in their first sermons—Acts 2:14ff.; 3:12ff.; 4:8ff.; 7:2ff.; and 10:34ff.)

It is not my purpose to delve into this problem of the actual fulfillment of prophecy. Rather, it is to point out that the general idea of the kingdom of God is a greater and wider reality than the messianic kingdom. The kingdom of God includes the kingdom of the Messiah, but it is by no means the equivalent of it.

Now is the time to summarize.

God himself wished the Israelites to think of him as their King and the King of the world. He wished them to think of his rule and kingdom as being ultimately invisible, but being nevertheless revealed in particular events, such as the Exodus. Thinking of God as King served to lead to a true experience of God and to helpful thoughts of him as the sovereign ruler of the universe, possessing all authority and power. Since God's rule was not wholly recognized and acknowledged by Israel and was rejected by other nations, the prophets spoke of an end to history following which there would be a new age in which the LORD would be truly King. However, within history they expected that the Mes-

siah's kingdom would be a true portrayal and part of
God's kingdom.

QUESTIONS FOR DISCUSSION

1. Since modern Westerners have not experienced absolute monarchy, can they truly experience and understand what "God is King" fully means?
2. If the language of symbolism is necessary to describe
events and experience beyond history, what are its
strengths and weaknesses in terms of communicating to
the modern mind?

2   THE TEACHING OF JESUS

Jesus only spoke of God specifically as "King" once
(Matthew 5:35), but he had much to say about the
"kingdom of God" or "kingdom of heaven." These expressions occur more frequently in the first three Gospels (with which we are here concerned) than in any
other parts of the Bible. Before we begin to understand
what they mean, a few explanatory words are necessary
concerning views held by the Jews at the time of Jesus.
Since the last book of the Old Testament was completed
400 years before his birth, Jesus had to bear in mind not
only what the authoritative Scriptures said about the
kingdom of God, but also the various interpretations of
this idea which were common in Judaism. This was necessary for him to communicate his development of the
Old Testament teaching in ways that would be meaningful to his hearers.

JEWISH VIEWS

We begin with the views of the rabbis who taught in the
synagogues both of Palestine and of the Jewish com-
munities of the Roman Empire. For them "kingdom of

God" or, rather, its equivalent, "kingdom of heaven" (they did not like to pronounce the divine name), was not a common expression. It was used in two basic ways. First of all, in a world of many deities the rabbis spoke of accepting "the yoke of the kingdom of God." They meant by this, accepting the God of Israel as the only true God; they were referring to a personal decision for monotheism. To believe in the God of the Jews as King and Lord was seen as a free and individual decision. Secondly, they spoke of the kingdom as wholly beyond history. God himself would end history by his intervention and then set up his kingdom; that is, he would rule absolutely. This rule of the Lord beyond history was a theme of prayers in the synagogue. For example:

Magnified and sanctified be his great name
in the world that he has created
according to his will.
May he establish his kingdom
in your lifetime and in your days
and in the lifetime of all the house of Israel,
even speedily and at a near time.

This is the kaddish prayer which was used before the time of Jesus and still is in use today.

Secondly, we need to be aware of the themes of those Jewish books which are usually called apocalyptic literature. This was produced in the period 200 B.C. to A.D. 100 by authors who used pseudonyms. It contained a particular and new view of God's action in the world on behalf of his covenant people. The belief was expressed that God would no more act redemptively in this present age, but would dramatically enter history to inaugurate the new age of his kingdom. Therefore, God was presented essentially as the God of the future, the God of the end of history.

Why was this literature produced? The answer lies in the fortunes of the Jewish people in a period which seemed to show that God had forgotten them. First of all, the Jews lived under the Seleucid (Greek) rulers from 200 B.C. to 164 B.C. Despite the heroism of the Maccabees (circa 166-160 B.C.) and a period of freedom under the Hasmonean rulers, they came under Roman rule in 63 B.C. God appeared not to act for them, even though there was much faithful keeping of the Law of Moses. Further, the voice of prophecy was silent. So, using the technique of descriptions of dreams and visions (supposedly from God), the writers of apocalyptic literature unveiled the future action of God in dramatic symbolism and powerful metaphor. God would enter history to close history and to set up his kingdom. Examples of these books are the *Assumption of Moses,* written just before the time of Jesus, and *The Testaments of the Twelve Patriarchs,* written in the second century B.C.

(It is important to note that the word "apocalyptic" is used not only of this literature, but of this technique of describing the intervention of God in human history in dramatic symbolism. Examples are found in the Bible of this technique—e.g., the books of Daniel and Revelation.)

Thirdly, moving from the realm of the imagination to the concrete political situation, it is necessary to note the views of the Zealots. They were a small, committed revolutionary movement whose aim was to rid their land of Roman soldiers. But their zeal was not exhausted in their struggle for political independence; they worked also for the coming of the rule of God. They believed that human initiative could hasten the beginning of the kingdom of God. This movement collapsed with the destruction of Jerusalem (A.D. 70) and Masada (A.D. 74) by the Romans. Simon, one of the twelve, had been a Zealot (Luke 6:15).

Common to these different approaches to the coming rule of God was the belief that evil powers—Satan, evil angels, and demons—were partially in control of the human situation. God was obviously not ruling in an observable and positive way, for the land of his covenant people was occupied by Gentiles and their armies. For reasons best known to himself, God, who still remained finally sovereign, had allowed this state of affairs to exist. However, in his good time he would reassert himself and gloriously triumph over all his spiritual and physical enemies. Then the rule of God would come.

Jesus knew the teaching concerning the kingdom given in the synagogue, apocalyptic literature, and by the Zealots. His method was not to enter into debate over the meaning of the kingdom of God. Rather, knowing what was taught within Judaism, but endorsing only what the Scriptures taught, Jesus proclaimed and embodied his own understanding of the kingdom. He did this in such a way that the careful listener could grasp the essentials of his message and know how it differed from that given by other rabbis or spokesmen, as well as how it fulfilled what the prophets of old had taught.

Before looking at the teaching of Jesus, a few comments are necessary on the Jewish expectation of the Messiah. The rabbis, who said little about the kingdom of heaven, said much about the coming of the Messiah and his kingdom or kingly rule. He was thought of as being a descendant of King David and a great liberator and conqueror. The kingdom of the Messiah would be the means of the change from the old order of human life to the new order of the kingdom of God.

In the apocalyptic literature when the Messiah is presented, it is in terms similar to the picture of the "son of man" in Daniel 7. He is one who comes to earth on the clouds of heaven to inaugurate the kingdom for God.

The Zealots looked to the appearance of the Messiah of the kingly line of David as the means of winning the war of liberation to set the Jewish people free, to establish the rule of righteousness, and to be the beginning of the arrival of the kingdom of God.

Obviously, in all strands of Jewish expectation there is a connection, even if it is not worked out coherently, between the Messiah and his kingdom and the kingdom of God.

MATTHEW, MARK, AND LUKE

The Greek words for king and kingdom are *basileus* and *basileia*. The latter has the breadth of meaning which we found in the Hebrew word *malkuth* and can refer to a kingdom or to kingly rule or to related ideas. As we noted, God is only called "King" once by Jesus (Matthew 5:35, citing Psalm 48:2; but see also Matthew 18:23 and 22:2-14), but Jesus himself is called king nearly forty times in the four Gospels. Here the sense is always the promised Messiah, the descendant of David, the predicted king of the Jews. See, for example, Matthew 2:2; 21:5; 25:34, 40; 27:11, 29, 37, 42; Mark 15:2, 9, 12, 18, 26, 32; Luke 19:38; 23:2, 3, 37, 38; John 1:49; 12:13, 15; 18:37, 39; 19:3, 12-14, 15, 19, 21.

In Matthew, the expression "kingdom of heaven" occurs thirty-three times, while "kingdom" or "kingdom of God" comes seventeen times. As Matthew was written for Jews, the use of "kingdom of heaven" reflects Jewish, rabbinic usage and the hesitancy to pronounce the divine name. Thus "kingdom of heaven" and "kingdom of God" mean the same. In Mark, "kingdom of

God" or "kingdom" is found fourteen times and in Luke thirty-nine times. Obviously, I cannot examine all the passages in which these phrases occur. So I shall seek to bring together under six headings the general thrust and meaning of the kingdom of God as implied by these passages.

God is active now, and his saving rule is operative among human beings.

Against the background of Jewish belief that God was absent from active involvement in human affairs, Jesus proclaimed that God was now present. At the beginning of his public ministry Jesus preached in Galilee, "The time is fulfilled, and the kingdom of God is at hand" (Mark 1:15; see also Matthew 4:17; 10:7; and Luke 10:9, 11). The words "at hand" could be paraphrased "has drawn near and is therefore very near now." For Jesus, God was near and was near in order to implement his rule of righteousness and salvation.

Further, against the background that the kingdom of God belongs only to the future, Jesus spoke of the kingdom as actually arriving and of breaking into human lives. In a controversy with the Pharisees, who accused Jesus of healing people by the power of Satan (whom they believed virtually ruled human affairs), Jesus made the important statement, "If it is by the Spirit of God that I cast out demons, then the kingdom of God has come upon you" (Matthew 12:28; compare Luke 11:20). The meaning is that the power of God is working in and through Jesus and when God's power causes healing and brings salvation, then God's rule has replaced the rule of Satan or demons in those lives. The "strong man" has been bound (v. 29).

In the presence of Jesus the devils trembled and confessed him as the Holy One of God (Mark 1:24; 5:7; etc.). People noticed that he spoke with a new kind of authority and clarity (Mark 1:27; 2:5; etc.). In his miracles, the power of Satan and death were broken and the life of the future kingdom of God experienced (Matthew 9:18ff.; Luke 7:11ff.). So he told his disciples privately, "Blessed are the eyes which see what you see! For I tell you that many prophets and kings desired to see what you see, and did not see it, and to hear what you hear, and did not hear it" (Luke 10:23).

Freedom, as brought by the ministry of Jesus, meant that the kingdom of God had broken the shackles of the kingdom of darkness; it meant that God's rule of grace and salvation had replaced the rule of Satan and sin.

The presence of the kingdom here and now is implied by the beatitudes of Jesus: "Blessed are the poor in spirit, for theirs is the kingdom of heaven" (Matthew 5:3). Or as Luke 6:20 has it, "Blessed are you poor, for yours is the kingdom of God." To be poor in the biblical sense means more than not to have riches; it is to be free from bondage to the value-systems of society, for they are not submitted to God. So only those are truly poor who have submitted to the saving rule of God and accepted it as "the pearl of great price" (Matthew 13:46).

Jesus also taught that the kingdom would break into human affairs in the near future. He told the disciples, "Truly, I say to you, there are some standing here who will not taste of death before they see that the kingdom of God has come with power" (Mark 9:1). He was referring to the glorious coming of the Holy Spirit to the disciples at the feast of Pentecost (Acts 2) and the subsequent mission of the Church in the Graeco-Roman world. For in the presence and power of the Spirit comes the rule and salvation of God. This mission was on a larger scale than the ministry of Jesus and his assistants in Palestine.

Thus, although Jesus did not share the view of the Zealots about the use of military force to assist in God's work, he did not hesitate to use the picture of an invading army to convey the idea of the entrance of God's power, rule, and salvation into human affairs. Like a powerful invader God is "at hand" (Mark 1:15), and he will come into the world "with power" (Mark 9:1).

To summarize, God—who for long years had been thought of as absent—was, said Jesus, waiting to enter into human lives in order to conquer sin and Satan and to bring in his salvation and wholeness.

This saving rule is present in Jesus and in his ministry.

By his perfect life of love and his trust in the heavenly Father, Jesus demonstrated that he lived in the kingdom of God. The LORD ruled his life. By his ministry, the ministry of God's servant, the Messiah, Jesus brought the kingdom of God into human experience as he cast out devils, healed the sick, made people whole, and forgave their sins. On one occasion, he gave to the Pharisees a clue to his identity when he told them, "The kingdom of God is not coming with signs to be observed; nor will they say, 'Lo, here it is,' or 'There!,' for behold, the kingdom of God is in the midst of you" (Luke 17:20, 21). Jesus, the Messiah, personally embodied the kingdom of God and, by the power of the Spirit, brought in or actualized the kingdom of God in concrete situations.

The defeat of Satan through the ministry of Jesus is also portrayed in vivid terms in Luke 10:1-20, which describes the mission of the seventy disciples Jesus sent out two by two. As the Messiah, he had the authority to share what belonged to him with chosen disciples who were in personal contact with him. Thus, he shared with these the powers of the kingdom. Sending them he said, "Whenever you enter a town and they receive you, eat what is set before you; heal the sick in it and say to them, 'The kingdom of God has come near to you.' But whenever you enter a town and they do not receive you, go into the streets and say, 'Even the dust of your town that clings to our feet, we wipe off against you; nevertheless know this, that the kingdom of God has come near.' I tell you, it shall be more tolerable on that day [the final day of judgment] for Sodom than for that town" (vv. 8-12).

When the disciples returned and announced that "even the demons are subject to us in your name," Jesus said, "I saw Satan fall like lightning from heaven" (v. 18). This is surely a dramatic way of saying that in the proclamation of the kingdom and the acts of healing and exorcisms, Jesus perceived the continuing defeat of Satan. The devil's kingdom was being overthrown.

Victory over the rule of Satan in human lives is one of the basic reasons why Jesus emphasized the importance of his suffering, death, and resurrection (see Mark 8:31ff., etc.). Through these he knew that he would win the decisive victory over death, sin, and Satan and so gloriously complete his work as Liberator and Savior. The saving rule of God embodied in him would triumph over all its enemies in his return from death to life, and then in his exaltation to the right hand of the Father. And being victorious, he would be able to send his Spirit to his disciples so that they would be able to share in his triumph (see John 14—16 and Ephesians 4:8-16).

*God's saving rule brings a new type of life, with new relation-
ships.*

Already the effects of the entrance of God's rule into
human lives have been noted. It brings wholeness and
salvation as Satan and evil are driven out. The enjoy-
ment of the blessings of God by those who are in God's
kingdom was emphasized by Jesus. In the Sermon on
the Mount, he told the disciples that as members of the
kingdom of God they would have no need to worry
about where their food and clothing came from. "Seek
first his kingdom and his righteousness, and all these
things shall be yours as well" (Matthew 6:33; see also
Luke 12:31). The inner peace and security of belonging
wholly to God was the internal blessing, and with it went
the knowledge that God would provide for all true
needs. "These things" are the basic necessities of life.

Becoming a disciple of Jesus and of the kingdom
could mean the loss of human friendships as a new life-
style was adopted. So Jesus taught, "Truly, I say to you,
there is no man who has left house or wife or brothers
or parents or children, for the sake of the kingdom of
God, who will not receive manifold more in this time,
and in the age to come eternal life" (Luke 18:29; see also
Mark 10:29, 30 and Matthew 19:29). The rule of God
demands sacrifices, even sacrifices of what are consid-
ered good things (e.g., staying with one's family), but the
compensations are high. Not only does the disciple of
the kingdom gain new brothers and sisters; he also gains
a new perspective on life and a new inner motivation
and happiness.

This new type of living was obviously different from
the rigorous and demanding religion of the Pharisees,
who had such a devotion to the letter of the Law of
Moses. Jesus told them, "Truly, I say to you, the tax
collectors and the harlots go into the kingdom of God

before you" (Matthew 21:31). On a later occasion he was very critical: "Woe to you, scribes and Pharisees, hypocrites! because you shut the kingdom of heaven against men; for you do neither enter yourselves, nor allow those who would enter to go in" (Matthew 23:13).

Included in the new life-style was the ability to forgive others. Jesus illustrated this not only in the petition of the Lord's Prayer—"Forgive us our debts as we also have forgiven our debtors"—but also in the parable in Matthew 18:23ff. This begins, "The kingdom of heaven may be compared to a king who wished to settle accounts with his servants. . . ." As the king began this task, one man was brought to him who owed him a massive amount of money. He had no hope whatsoever of paying this back and so, according to the custom of those times, the king ordered that he and his family be sold as slaves. But the man begged for mercy, and in compassion the king canceled his debt so that he had nothing to pay. However, as this man was going home he met another man who owed him a rather small amount of money and asked for more time to pay the debt. This time was not given, and the second man was put into debtor's prison.

When the king heard of this action, he recalled the man whose great debt he had canceled and reversed the decision he had made. The debtor was flung into prison. The point of the story, said Jesus, is that genuine forgiveness should be found in the life of disciples of the kingdom, for they have had a tremendous debt of sin canceled by God himself. If they do not exhibit such forgiveness, they cannot expect mercy from God at the Last Judgment. Those in whom the God of love and forgiveness reigns should readily forgive others who wrong them.

Those in whom God's salvation, forgiveness, and rule

are present find that God is not only the King, he is also the Father who cares for his adopted children. Jesus said, "If you then, who are evil, know how to give good gifts to your children, how much more will your Father who is in heaven give good things to those who ask him!" (Matthew 7:11; cf. Matthew 6:6-8).

With God as Father and other disciples as brothers and sisters, to be in God's kingdom now is to be truly happy, truly blessed, despite possible poverty and loss of human prestige. It is to possess a life now which will survive death and continue to grow in the life of the age to come. It is to be ruled by a loving heavenly Father.

God always takes the initiative, for it is his saving rule; but he calls for the response of the individual.

Jesus taught his disciples to pray, "Thy kingdom come, thy will be done, on earth as it is in heaven" (Matthew 6:10). Certainly he did not agree with the Zealots that the activity of men could actually bring in the kingdom. He taught that "it is your Father's good pleasure to give you the kingdom" (Luke 12:32; cf. Matthew 25:34). To possess the kingdom is, as Zacchaeus came to know, to have God's salvation (Luke 19:9).

Yet Jesus did teach that there was a proper human response. If God's rule stands like an invading army on the outside of human lives setting conditions for entry, then those conditions have to be met. Here are some of the conditions which Jesus mentioned:

"If your eye causes you to sin, pluck it out; it is better for you to enter the kingdom of God with one eye than with two eyes to be thrown into Gehenna" (Mark 9:47). Here the idea via the hyperbole is that the disciple of the kingdom should be prepared to sacrifice anything in order to let the rule of God fill his life completely.

Later Jesus said, "Truly, I say to you, whoever does not receive the kingdom of God like a child shall not enter it" (Mark 10:15). Precisely what Jesus meant by being childlike is not clear. Perhaps he referred to the need for a person to learn to think of God as his heavenly Father, to be so trustful of him as to call him "Abba" (= Daddie). To be dependent on riches made it virtually impossible to trust God as Father. So Jesus taught, "How hard it will be for those who have riches to enter into the kingdom of God. . . . It is easier for a camel to go through the eye of a needle than for a rich man to enter the kingdom of God" (Mark 10:23-25).

During the week in Jerusalem before the Crucifixion, Jesus had a happy encounter with a pious lawyer. The man appeared to have realized the nature of true religion, for he confessed that to love God and man is far more important than offering animal sacrifices. Jesus commended him and said, "You are not far from the kingdom of God" (Mark 12:34). The lawyer was being encouraged to set himself free from the traditional ideas of the Pharisees in order that he could be in a position to submit to the loving rule of God.

Submission to God's kingdom is not a temporary activity or something that is done for a change. Jesus said that "No one who puts his hand to the plow and looks back (or "keeps looking back") is fit for the kingdom of God" (Luke 9:62). The kingdom demands an irrevocable decision. It also demands a radical decision, leading to extreme change. This is the meaning of the two seemingly odd statements of Jesus: "From the days of John the Baptist until now the kingdom of heaven has suffered violence, and men of violence take it by force" (Matthew 11:12); and, "The law and prophets were until John; since then the good news of the kingdom of

God is preached, and every one enters it violently"
(Luke 16:16). The kingdom of God is so utterly different from any earthly reality that it makes a demand
which may be described in terms of violence, in that it
does violence to normal ideas of decisions and their importance. Yet, as Jesus made clear, membership brings
joy—not joy which is here today and gone tomorrow,
but joy which lasts forever.

God's rule will be fully implemented at the close of history.

In harmony with the teaching of the prophets of the
old covenant, Jesus looked for the fullness and universality of the kingdom of God outside history; that is,
after the close of this age. The events which he saw as
linking the present age with the fullness of the kingdom
in the age to come were his own return to earth in power
and glory and the judgment of the nations and peoples
of the earth. In the Sermon on the Mount, he spoke of
entering the future kingdom of heaven, but reminded
his hearers that only they who did the will of the Father
in this age would enter into the kingdom in the age to
come (Matthew 7:21ff.). Of the universality of the future kingdom he had this to say as he compared it to a
celebration banquet: "Many will come from east and
west and sit at table with Abraham, Isaac, and Jacob in
the kingdom of heaven . . ." (Matthew 8:11). At the end
of his explanation of his parable of the man who sowed
good seed by day and his enemy who sowed weeds by
night, Jesus spoke of the great happiness of those who
inhabit the future kingdom: "The righteous will shine
like the sun in the kingdom of their Father" (Matthew
13:43).

Many times Jesus spoke of his return to earth at the
end of the present age. Often he described himself as

"the Son of Man," a phrase probably taken by him from Daniel 7 where one "like a son of man" is described as receiving a kingdom from God. It is in these passages that Jesus, using the expression "Son of Man," makes use of language which is similar to the apocalyptic literature of Judaism. So, Matthew 24, Mark 13, and Luke 21, which contain a discourse by Jesus concerning the fall of Jerusalem (A.D. 70) and his own second coming, have been called "the little apocalypse," for they use the language of symbolism and imagery and are not meant to be read as literally true statements of fact. Here is an example: "Immediately after the tribulation of those days the sun will be darkened, and the moon will not give its light, and the stars will fall from heaven, and the powers of the heavens will be shaken; and then will appear the sign of the Son of man in heaven, and then all the tribes of the earth will mourn, and they will see the Son of man coming on the clouds of heaven with power and great glory . . ." (Matthew 24:29ff.). The three parables in Matthew 25 (ten virgins, the talents, and the sheep and goats) all refer to the events at the close of the present age. In the parable of the final judgment (sheep and goats) Jesus, pictured as a monarch on a throne dispensing justice, says to the faithful, "Come, O blessed of my Father, inherit the kingdom prepared for you from the foundation of the world" (Matthew 25:34).

Jesus himself experienced the equivalent of the fullness of the future kingdom of God when after his crucifixion he rose from the dead and ascended into heaven. In the presence of the Father and the holy angels, Jesus experienced the fullness of God's power and rule. This is what he had in mind when he told his disciples at the Last Supper, "Truly, I say to you, I shall

not drink again of the fruit of the vine until that day
when I drink it new in the kingdom of God" (Mark
14:25). At this stage, we recall, his resurrection from the
dead was only three days away.

To understand God's present, saving rule is to grasp a mystery.

As we noted in the study of the Old Testament, the
arrival of the kingdom is presented there in terms of a
single, cataclysmic event. For example, in the vision
recorded in Daniel 2 the kingdom of God, like a great
stone, crushes all the kingdoms of the world. Having
this understanding, devout Jews like John the Baptist
were confused by Jesus who claimed that the kingdom
had arrived though there was no visible change in the
political order of the day. This is why John sent messengers to Jesus with questions for him to answer (see Matthew 11:2ff. and Luke 7:18ff.). The reply of Jesus was
that the kingdom was present, but that instead of crush-
ing the kingdoms of the world, it was defeating the invisible but real kingdom of Satan. Defeat of the kingdoms
of the world would follow at the end of the age. The
arrival of the kingdom of God here and now to remove
the spiritual rule of Satan in human lives is basically
what Jesus meant by the "mystery" or "secret" of the
kingdom (Matthew 13:11; Mark 4:11).

Some of his parables illustrate this "mystery." It is a
mystery that the kingdom of *almighty* God has arrived
and finite people can actually reject it. The parable of
the four types of soil in Matthew 13:1-9, 18-23 shows
that people may, and do, resist the offer of God's saving
rule in their lives. It is also a mystery that God's kingdom exists in the world alongside the kingdom of Satan
and the kingdoms of men, and often appears to be
weaker than they. The parable of the wheat and the

tares in Matthew 13:24-30 shows that this state of affairs will prevail until the end of this evil age. Furthermore, it is a mystery that God's kingdom is present in the here and now, but in a most insignificant manner. The parables of the grain of mustard seed and of the leaven in the dough (Matthew 13:31-33) contrast the insignificance in the present evil age with the universal significance at the end of the age; the difference is as between a tiny seed and a large shrub or between a minute piece of yeast and the resultant large piece of dough or bread.

Therefore, the mystery may be summed up in the claim that in the man of Nazareth, Jesus the traveling rabbi, and in his ministry the great and glorious future kingdom of God was a present reality as it did battle with the kingdom of Satan.

JOHN

Before providing a general summary, a few comments on the Gospel of John are perhaps necessary. The phrase "kingdom of God" occurs only twice in this Gospel and the two are in one context, the record of the conversation of Jesus with Nicodemus. Jesus said to him, "Truly, truly, I say to you, unless one is born anew [or from above] he cannot see the kingdom of God" (John 3:3). (This is similar to the statement by Jesus to his disciples: "Truly, I say to you, unless you turn and become like children, you will never enter the kingdom of heaven" [Matthew 18:3].) When Nicodemus appeared to misunderstand what had been said, Jesus further explained, "Truly, truly, I say to you, unless one is born of water and of the Spirit, he cannot enter the kingdom of God. That which is born of the flesh is flesh, and that which is born of the Spirit is spirit" (verses 5, 6). This emphasis on the work of the Holy Spirit as the

bringer of the kingdom reminds us of such passages as
Matthew 12:28. From the conversation of Jesus with
Nicodemus, two themes concerning the kingdom may
be deduced. First of all, the kingdom of God is not a
reality which human beings can create, for it comes
through the initiative and work of God himself. Secondly, the kingdom of God arrives in the here and now,
bringing a new order and type of life—"eternal life."

At his trial, Jesus spoke of the kingdom as his own
kingdom. He said, "My kingship [or kingdom] is not of
this world; if my kingship were of this world, my servants would fight, that I might not be handed over to
the Jews; but my kingship is not from the world"
(18:36). This practice is also found in Matthew and
Luke; see Matthew 13:41, 20:21 and Luke 22:29, 23:42.
The word *basileia,* as we noted earlier, may be translated
as "reign," "rule," or "kingship" as well as "kingdom."
Therefore, Jesus may here have been speaking of the
nature of his messiahship ("kingship") as not being like
that of the rule of an earthly king, or of his kingdom as
not being like an earthly kingdom.

The virtual absence of the phrase "kingdom of God"
in this Gospel has led scholars to suggest that the expressions "eternal life" (occurring nineteen times) and
"life" (occurring seventeen times) are at least partial
synonyms for "kingdom." We may affirm that there are
grounds for this suggestion in the synoptic Gospels
where the kingdom of God means, as we have noted, the
experience in the here and now of God's saving rule and
eternal salvation. In one conversation, that with the rich
young ruler, Jesus actually identified being in the kingdom with having eternal life (see Luke 18:18ff.; compare verse 18 with verses 24, 25. The same incident is
recorded also in Matthew 19:16ff. and Mark 10:17ff.).

In the Gospel of John we find that eternal life has the following characteristics:

1. It includes life beyond death—see 5:28, 29.

2. It is a rich quality of life experienced in the here and now of this evil age—see 5:24; 6:40, 54. It is an abundant life—see 10:10.

3. It is life which God alone can and does give—see 6:32-35; 10:27, 28; 17:2.

4. The life is received by *believing* sinners—see John 3:14-16, 36; 5:24; 20:30, 31.

The reader of this Gospel knows that such life is none other than God's life—the life of the Father through the Son and Holy Spirit, placed in the heart of the believer. It is the life of the future kingdom of God experienced now; it is thus the kingdom of God in the lives of believers.

Before leaving John's Gospel, we must notice briefly another feature which relates to the kingdom of God while not specifically using the expression. The feature is the distinctive teaching on the Holy Spirit found in chapters 14—16. One way of interpreting this teaching is to say that Jesus taught that the Spirit would bring the kingdom of God into people's lives through the ministry of the apostles and the churches. At the request of the Son, the Father would send the Spirit, who would continue the work begun on earth by the Son. This would certainly include the bringing of eternal life to believing, repentant sinners. On the day of Pentecost, the Holy Spirit came to the apostles and disciples and through their ministry, conducted in the power of the Spirit, thousands entered the kingdom of God. Entering, they received the same eternal life which those received who, during the ministry of Jesus, believed his word.

To summarize the Gospel of John's contributions,

though there are only two recorded statements of Jesus which include the expression "kingdom of God," there is teaching in the Gospel from Jesus which is synonymous with or equivalent to teaching in the other Gospels. Further, in the teaching on the Holy Spirit as the one who would come to the disciples after the exaltation of Jesus, there is a new dimension added which, as we shall see, is taken up especially by Paul in his teaching concerning the kingdom.

SUMMARY

Jesus never gave any systematic teaching on the subject of kingdom, and he used a cluster of images or models to convey his message. He spoke of the rule of God on many occasions, and from these I have drawn the various principles expounded above. It is probably true to say that his primary aim was not to get over a perfectly clear concept of the kingdom, but rather to give people a sense of the nearness of God, the LORD, and to evoke a response to God from them. This is not to say that he did not possess or could not have given what we would call a precise theological definition. Rather, it is to say that the teaching and activity of Jesus was aimed at bringing people into contact with the living God and causing them to live in obedience to his rule.

How, then, did the message of Jesus concerning the kingdom differ from that of his Jewish contemporaries? First of all, the kingdom was for him a living, dynamic reality, making an immediate demand on people and offering them salvation and wholeness now. Here he differed from the Rabbis who equated the kingdom with the profession of monotheism in a world of polytheism. Unlike them, he could tell repentant sinners, "The kingdom has come upon you."

Secondly, for Jesus the coming of the kingdom was wholly the initiative of God. Certainly people had to respond, but they only responded to the movement of God toward them; they could not cause God to move to them. Here he differed especially from the Zealots who believed that by armed rebellion they could help to usher in the rule of God. Zealots could not say as Jesus did, "Render to Caesar the things that are Caesar's" (Mark 12:13ff.).

Thirdly, for Jesus the kingdom was a reality to be known and experienced in the present as well as in the future. The experience of the kingdom now was a foretaste of the kingdom to come. God was not absent, but present as the ruling and gracious God. Here Jesus differed with the views of the writers of apocalyptic literature, for whom God would remain absent until the end of the age. Certainly Jesus used apocalyptic imagery when describing the events leading to the end of history and the entrance of God's kingdom in its fullness (e.g., Mark 13), but he also spoke of the rule of God in the here and now.

What can be asserted positively is that Jesus developed the teaching of the Old Testament writers on the kingdom of God. First of all, he began to fulfill in himself and his activity the prophecies about the coming of the Messiah and the kingdom of the Messiah. In terms of the future rule of God over the whole cosmos, Jesus also developed the Old Testament material by teaching concerning himself as the Son of man returning to the earth in power and great glory to judge the living and the dead. What was truly new in the teaching of Jesus was the emphasis on the kingdom being present, the kingdom coming through the activity (miracles, exorcisms, etc.) of Jesus. This is what he meant when he talked about the mystery of the kingdom being revealed to his disciples (Mark 4:11, 12). While the Old Testament psalmists and prophets knew of the general, providential rule of God over creation and history and of his involvement in saving action for Israel, they did not know the immediacy and the power of the rule of God in the here and now which Jesus exhibited in himself and brought into the lives of those to whom he ministered. The mystery of the kingdom is the coming of the kingdom into history in advance of its fullness at the end of time.

QUESTIONS FOR DISCUSSION

1. What view of the kingdom of God is found in the parables of Mark 4 and Matthew 13?
2. "The kingdom is present" and "The kingdom will be revealed." Is it possible to reconcile these two approaches?

3   THE APOSTOLIC TEACHING

According to the Synoptic Gospels, Jesus proclaimed
the kingdom of God as his central message. This being
so, the question occurs to the thoughtful Bible reader:
Why did the apostles apparently say little about the
kingdom? In the Acts of the Apostles the phrase occurs
seven times, and in Paul's fourteen letters it occurs fourteen times. Did the apostles not share the belief of Jesus
about the kingdom? The answer is that they certainly
did share his views; indeed, they wanted only to teach
what he taught, but they understood that teaching in the
light of two great redeeming and saving actions of God:
Jesus had gloriously risen from the dead and ascended
into heaven; and, the Father had sent the Holy Spirit in
the name of Jesus Christ to the waiting disciples (Acts 2).
Jesus was now the exalted Messiah and Lord, and the
Holy Spirit was present in the believing community, the
church, and working in the world. So instead of speaking only about the kingdom of God, the apostles spoke
also of Christ the King (that is, the Lordship of Jesus
Christ, who sits at the right hand of the Father), and of
the power of the Holy Spirit, who continues Christ's
work in the world.

We shall look first at the Acts of the Apostles and then at the teaching of Paul. As the verses in which the phrase "kingdom of God" occurs are few, I shall first list these. I shall also list the few references to the LORD or Christ as King. This may appear tedious, but it is necessary in order to gain a clear view of the apostolic teaching. Having done this, I shall examine the relation of the Lordship of Christ and the power of the Holy Spirit to the kingdom of God. Finally, I shall look briefly at the teaching of John, the author of the last book of the New Testament.

ACTS OF THE APOSTLES

Here, first of all, are the verses:

1. Referring to the Gospel of Luke, which he had already written, and to the resurrection of Jesus which he had recorded, Luke wrote that Jesus *presented himself alive after his passion by many proofs, appearing to them during forty days, and speaking of the kingdom of God* (1:3).

2. Philip was preaching in Samaria, and Luke described this as preaching *good news about the kingdom of God and the name of Jesus Christ* (8:12). Here the definite link between the kingdom and the ascended Jesus, now the exalted Messiah and Lord, is made.

3. As Paul and Barnabas passed through the towns of Lystra, Iconium, and Antioch, they *strengthened the souls of the disciples, exhorting them to continue in the faith, and saying that through many tribulations we must enter the kingdom of God* (14:22). The common lot of the first Christians was persecution, which was interpreted as suffering with Christ. Here the idea is that fellowship with God and God's rule in human lives is achieved in the context of tribulation.

4. Paul entered the synagogue in Ephesus and *for*

three months spoke boldly, arguing and pleading about the kingdom of God (19:8). As Paul was addressing Jews, we are to understand that he was attempting to show them from their Scriptures how God's rule now in human lives and his universal rule in the future was intimately associated with the fact that Jesus of Nazareth is Messiah and Lord.

5. In his farewell message to the elders of the church in Ephesus Paul said, *I know that all you among whom I have gone preaching the kingdom will see my face no more* (20:25). The kingdom is that which has drawn near and become a reality in and through Jesus the Messiah.

6. In Rome, Paul addressed his fellow-Jews *testifying to the kingdom of God and trying to convince them about Jesus both from the law of Moses and from the prophets* (28:23). Again Paul is arguing that God's redemptive rule and saving grace have come into the world already, in anticipation of future fullness, in and through Jesus.

7. Also in Rome, Paul taught for two years and he welcomed all who came to his lodging, *preaching the kingdom of God and teaching about the Lord Jesus Christ . . .* (28:31). Paul could not teach or preach about the kingdom without preaching about Jesus, the resurrected and exalted Messiah. The two belonged inextricably together in his thought.

These passages make clear that the apostles were interpreting the kingdom of God in light of Jesus, the Christ and Lord. This is confirmed if we look at the earliest sermons of the Church, recorded in Acts 2:14-36; 2:38, 39; 3:12-26; 10:34-43. According to Mark, Jesus entered Galilee at the beginning of his public ministry and proclaimed, "The time is fulfilled, and the kingdom of God is at hand; repent, and believe in the gospel" (1:15). According to Luke's reporting of the first sermons, the following were the themes of the apostolic good news in the first sermons:

1. The prophecies of the Old Testament are fulfilled, and the new age is a reality through the coming of Jesus.

2. Jesus was born of the line of King David.

3. Jesus died as the prophets had foretold in order to deliver us from sin and the present evil age.

4. Jesus was buried and therefore truly dead.

5. Jesus rose from death on the third day, as the prophets had foretold.

6. Jesus is now exalted to the right hand of the Father as Messiah, Lord, and Son of God.

7. Jesus will come again as the Judge of the world.

8. Forgiveness is offered to those who repent and believe this good news.

In his public ministry, Jesus called upon people to believe and accept his words about God and his kingdom. The apostles called upon people to believe in Jesus himself (which of course includes believing what he said). At the center of the message of Jesus was the kingdom of God and at the center of the message of the apostles is the message of Jesus, the Messiah, who has died and is now exalted to heaven. In other words, God's perfect rule and God's entering into human history has happened in Jesus of Nazareth. This saving rule becomes a living experience in the life of a human being when he believes on Jesus, receiving him as Messiah and Lord.

The Acts of the Apostles make clear that the saving rule of God is realized in the individual life by the presence of the Holy Spirit, who brings power and blessing. The Holy Spirit, who came to the disciples on the day of Pentecost with such amazing signs, is presented in Acts as the One who embodies God's saving power and rule

(1:8; 2:4, 33; 8:19; etc.) and who brings wholeness and blessing (3:6; 13:52; etc.). So the kingdom of God is experienced now through belief in the Lord Jesus and by receiving the gift of the Holy Spirit.

There is also the conviction running through the whole book of Acts that God is the King of the world in the sense that he rules both nature and the history of the nations—see, for example, 17:22-31. The word "King" is not, however, used of the LORD.

When Jesus cast out demons and healed people by the power of the Spirit, he said that the kingdom of God had come upon them (Matthew 12:28). In the Acts (e.g., 3:6), the healings are attributed to the power of the name of the Lord Jesus (= the power of the Spirit). The kingly rule of God thereby replaced the rule of Satan and sin.

THE LETTERS OF PAUL

Here, first of all, are the verses:

1. There was some disagreement in the church at Rome over what food and drink were permissible for Christians. In giving advice, Paul said that the *kingdom of God is not food and drink but righteousness and peace and joy in the Holy Spirit* (14:17). Here he was stating that the primary fact for Christians to ask themselves is whether God rules in their lives, and the evidence of that rule is the presence of righteousness, peace, and joy, which come from the presence of the Holy Spirit. The kingdom is an inner reality, the power and presence of the Holy Spirit in the heart producing holiness of life.

2. In order to understand what a reality is, it is sometimes important to say what it is not. So Paul told the Corinthians that *the kingdom of God does not consist in talk but in power* (1 Corinthians 4:20). The presence of the

power of the Spirit in a life enables the believer not merely to talk but to live and act for God, which means to suffer indignity and persecution for Christ's sake.

3. In a further negative statement Paul said, *Do you not know that the unrighteous will not inherit the kingdom of God?* (1 Corinthians 6:9) and followed it by,

4. *Do not be deceived; neither the immoral, nor idolaters, nor adulterers, nor thieves, nor the greedy, nor drunkards, nor revilers, nor robbers will inherit the kingdom of God* (1 Corinthians 6:9, 10). The rule of God is the opposite of unrighteous and immoral behavior.

5. After the second coming of Christ, there will be the resurrection of the dead. *Then comes the end when he (Christ) delivers the kingdom to God the Father after destroying every rule and every authority and power* (1 Corinthians 15:24). This belongs to that which shall be at the end of human history, when the kingdom of God comes in fullness. From his exaltation at the ascension until his second coming there is a real sense in which Christ, the exalted Lord, is King of God's kingdom, and this is what is spoken of here.

6. Since the kingdom of God in its fullness lies beyond the resurrection of the dead, then *flesh and blood cannot inherit the kingdom of God* (1 Corinthians 15:50).

7. Paul told the Galatians much the same as what he told the Corinthians. Those whose lives are dominated by sinful desires are not in the kingdom of God. *The works of the flesh are plain: fornication, impurity . . . anger, selfishness . . . envy . . . and the like. . . . Those who do such things shall not inherit the kingdom of God* (Galatians 5:19-21).

8. And he had the same type of advice for the Ephesians. *No fornicator or impure man . . . has any inheritance in the kingdom of Christ and of God* (Ephesians 5:5). Here we have the interesting parallelism of the kingdom of

Christ and of God. This is similar to 1 Corinthians 15:24 and reminds us that now Christ, the Lord, rules from the right hand of the Father as King.

9. A further reference to the kingdom as belonging to Christ is found in Colossians. *He (the Father) has delivered us from the dominion of darkness and transferred us to the kingdom of his beloved Son, in whom we have redemption, the forgiveness of sins* (1:13). God's rule in human lives comes to Christians through Jesus Christ in the power of the Spirit. By the design and will of the Father, and through the saving work of Christ, salvation and forgiveness is won for them, and this is applied to them by the Holy Spirit. Until the end of history Christ, the eternal Son, rules as the Father's vicegerent, and so the kingdom is his.

10. Paul did not labor alone in proclaiming the kingdom of God, and he described those who worked with him as *fellow workers for the kingdom of God* (Colossians 4:11). Is Paul saying that human labor can actually bring in the rule of God? No! He is saying that God has chosen men to be the means whereby news of the kingdom and the blessings of the kingdom are made known on earth. The reign and rule is God's, but he employs servants.

11. When Paul was in Thessalonica, he urged and encouraged the Christians *to lead a life worthy of God, who calls you into his own kingdom and glory* (1 Thessalonians 2:12). By the new birth, believers are born into the kingdom of God, and they will experience the fullness and the glory of the kingdom at the end of time.

12. Under trial and persecution, the Christians in Thessalonica had remained steadfast in the faith. Thus he commented: *This is evidence of the righteous judgment of God that you may be made worthy of the kingdom of God, for which you are suffering* (2 Thessalonians 1:5). By the power of the Spirit, the Christians had remained faith-

ful during tribulation and had thereby revealed that the kingly rule of God was in their lives and that they would be members of that kingdom whose fullness was yet to dawn.

13. Expressing praise, Paul exclaimed: *To the King of ages, immortal, invisible, the only God, be honor and glory for ever and ever. Amen* (1 Timothy 1:17). Here the Old Testament doctrine of God as King is reaffirmed. He is the Lord of history.

14. In describing the same God, he wrote of *the blessed and only Sovereign, the King of kings and Lord of lords, who alone has immortality and dwells in unapproachable light, whom no man has ever seen or can see* (1 Timothy 6:15, 16).

15. In writing to Timothy, Paul solemnly charged him: *I charge you in the presence of God and of Christ Jesus who is to judge the living and the dead, and by his appearing and his kingdom . . .* (2 Timothy 4:1). Paul's appeal was against the background of two well-known truths—the second coming of Christ in power and glory, and the fullness of the future kingdom of God.

16. The certainty of the future kingdom is also found in the final reference: *The Lord will rescue me from every evil and save me for his heavenly kingdom* (2 Timothy 4:18).

The themes found in these verses must now be brought together to gain a coherent picture of Paul's view of the kingdom. First of all, we note that following the teaching of Jesus, Paul understood the kingdom as having both a present and a future dimension. The reality of the rule of God in the here and now is taught in Romans 14:17 and Colossians 1:13, while the hope of the future glorious kingdom is found in 1 Corinthians 6:9, 10; 2 Timothy 4:1, 18.

Secondly, Paul placed great emphasis, as did Jesus in the Sermon on the Mount, on purity of life, on righteousness and holiness, as evidence of membership in the kingdom and as proof that God ruled by the Holy Spirit in the heart. This is clear from Romans 14:17; 1 Corinthians 6:9, 10; Galatians 5:21; Ephesians 5:5; 1 Thessalonians 2:12; and 2 Thessalonians 1:5. It seems that Paul makes this ethical emphasis his strongest theme in speaking of the kingdom.

Finally, Paul follows the lead of Jesus himself (see John 18:36) to speak of the kingdom as being Christ's kingdom; see 1 Corinthians 15:24; Ephesians 5:5; Colossians 1:13. As the exalted Lord, Jesus Christ rules the kingdom of God as the vicegerent of the Father, who remains King of the universe. As this teaching on the Lordship of Christ is very important for Paul, we shall look at it now in more detail.

THE LORDSHIP OF JESUS

To preach Jesus as Lord was central to Paul's understanding of the good news, and to confess Jesus as Lord was central to his understanding of the reception of the salvation of God. Here are several strong statements from Paul.

If you confess with your lips that Jesus is Lord and believe in your heart that God raised him from the dead, you will be saved (Romans 10:9).

No one can say "Jesus is Lord" except by the Holy Spirit (1 Corinthians 12:3).

For what we preach is not ourselves, but Jesus Christ as Lord, with ourselves as your servants for Jesus' sake (2 Corinthians 4:5).

Then, for the complete understanding of Paul's view of Jesus as Lord, there is the powerful passage found in Philippians 2:6-11, here quoted from the *Good News Bible*.

He always had the nature of God,

but he did not think that by force
He should try to become equal with God.
Instead of this, of his own free will he
gave up all he had,
and took the nature of a servant.
He became like man
and appeared in human likeness.
He was humble and walked the path
of obedience all the way to death—
his death on the cross.
For this reason God raised him to the
highest place above
and gave him the name that is greater
than any other name.
And so, in honor of the name of Jesus
all beings in heaven, on earth, and
in the world below
will fall on their knees,
and all will openly proclaim that Jesus
Christ is Lord
to the glory of God the Father.

Here Paul depicts the exaltation of Jesus Christ (in resurrection and ascension) following his great humiliation in leaving the glory of heaven to become a human being and to suffer for the sins of the world.

The picture of the exalted Jesus sitting or standing at the right hand of the Father (Acts 7:56; Ephesians 1:20) is based on Psalm 110:1 where the LORD tells the Messiah to sit by his side until the time comes to finally conquer all his foes. It is a simple way of stating that Jesus, the exalted Lord, rules as the vicegerent of the Father. For this present age, the Father has committed rule into the hands of the exalted Lord. We may understand the rule of Christ as including all that the Father rules. This is why Paul can make such statements as "Christ is before all things, and in him all things hold together" (Colossians 1:17). It is basic to the Old Testament and to the Gospels that God is ultimately in charge of the world; that is, he is the God who guides history and sustains the creation. Paul referred to God as the King of the ages (1 Timothy 1:17) and the King of kings and Lord of lords (1 Timothy 6:15). As the eternal Son of God, Jesus Christ shares in this general rule with the Father. However, the essential point about his new name of "Lord" is that his special and specific reign is what Paul calls "the reign of grace" (Romans 5 and 6).

With Jesus, who both embodied and proclaimed the kingdom of God, now absent from earth and present in heaven, Paul faced the question, "How is God's kingdom known on earth now among sinful people?" His answer, put as simply as possible, went something like this:

1. The exaltation of Jesus meant that he had conquered all those foes who prohibited the rule of God in human lives. He had triumphed over sin, death, Satan, and hell and, like a victorious king, had gloriously ascended into heaven carrying the spoils of his victory. (See Paul's picture of Jesus as the triumphant warrior-king in Ephesians 4:8ff. where he adapts Psalm 68:18.)

2. He has conquered these foes not for his own good, but for all who will respond to the call of the gospel. He is the Messiah, the Mediator, and the Savior; and what he accomplished, he accomplished for all.

3. From heaven as God's vicegerent, Jesus continues the work he did in Palestine as the Messiah on earth. He does this by the power of the Holy Spirit who works through chosen servants in the world (Ephesians 4:11ff.; cf. John 16:8ff.). He extends his rule over individuals through the word of his witnesses (2 Corinthians 4:5; 5:18-20). This word is powerful and liberates human beings. "I am not ashamed of the gospel," wrote

Paul; "it is the power of God for salvation to every one who has faith" (Romans 1:16).

4. By the power of the Word and the Spirit, the victory achieved by Christ is realized in human lives as they respond to the Good News. The Spirit enters human hearts, which then produce the fruit of the Spirit (Galatians 5:22, 23). The kingdom has arrived when the Spirit lives in human hearts, for the "kingdom of God is . . . righteousness and peace and joy in the Holy Spirit" (Romans 14:17).

5. Thus, the reign of Christ now is his rule by Word and Spirit in individual believers and in the fellowship of believers, whom the Spirit brings together in the body of Christ. Christ is the Lord or King both of the individual and of the Church (Ephesians 1:22, 23; Colossians 1:18-20).

6. The presence of the Spirit in human hearts is an anticipation of the fullness of the future kingdom of God. Paul used two words in Ephesians 1:13, 14 to describe this divine gift of anticipation. He said it was like a seal, the seal on official documents and letters, and it was a seal executed by God. Also, it was like an initial deposit, a down payment which was the first installment and the promise of more to come, and God made this deposit. The salvation enjoyed by the believer in the here and now is a foretaste of the greater and fuller experience of God's love in the kingdom to come. The life of God which truly belongs to the future is enjoyed in the present. So Paul's teaching here corresponds with that of Jesus, who taught that God gives now the gift of eternal life (John 3:16; etc.).

One more aspect of Paul's teaching on the Lordship needs to be explained. He believed that this reign of grace in believing sinners and in the church would continue to the end of history, to the judgment of the world, when Christ would return to earth. "Then comes the end when he delivers the kingdom to God the Father after destroying every rule and every authority and power" (1 Corinthians 15:24). At this point his work of Messiah, Lord, Mediator, and Savior will be completed, and he will rule henceforth as the eternal Son of God, a member of the holy and blessed Trinity.

So we see that Paul had two pictures or two models in his mind as he thought about the divine kingdom. First, basing his thinking on the teaching of the Old Testament and the teaching of Jesus, he spoke of the kingdom of God (the Father) as the rule of God in individuals in the here and now, as well as universally at the end of the age. Also he spoke of God as King, the Ruler of history and nature. Then, secondly, he spoke of the kingdom of Christ in terms of the Lordship of Christ, as being the way in which the rule of God the Father is executed from the time of the ascension of Jesus until his return to earth in power and glory. The picture of God the Father as Ruler is the primary picture, but as an ambassador of Christ Paul wrote more fully about the kingdom of Christ. The roots of Paul's doctrine of the kingship or kingdom of Christ are the Old Testament prophecies about the kingdom of the Messiah (e.g., Isaiah 11; Psalms 2 and 110) and the hints which Jesus himself gave about himself and his kingdom (e.g., John 18:36).

THE REVELATION OF JOHN

A prominent theme of this book is the victory of the exalted Jesus (in which his church shares) over all his material and spiritual foes. It was written at a time when Christians were being persecuted because they would not submit to the demand from the Roman State that the Emperor be worshiped as "Lord and God." To John

on the island of Patmos, God granted visions of the
certain triumph of Jesus Christ. Thus, throughout the
book Jesus Christ is pictured as the mighty Victor and
the great Conqueror. His vanquished foes are death,
Hades (the abyss), the dragon (Satan), the beast (Roman
power), the false prophet (the organization behind the
cult of emperor worship), and those who actually worship the beast. As Jesus Christ is the Victor in the name
of God, we shall not be surprised to find that both the
Father and Jesus (the Son) are called King and worshiped as such. Here are the verses which portray God
or Christ as King and speak of their kingdom.

1. John explained that his suffering was in the name
of and for the sake of the saving rule of God: *I John, your
brother, who share with you in Jesus the tribulation and the
kingdom and the patient endurance . . .* (1:9).

2. He saw the rule of the exalted Jesus at the Father's
right hand as meaning there would be ultimate, certain
victory for the Christian cause: *The kingdom of the world
has become the kingdom of our Lord and of his Christ, and he
shall reign for ever and ever* (11:15).

3. The reign of the exalted Christ and his triumph is
also the triumph of God, and so the heavenly choir
sang: *We give thanks to thee, Lord God Almighty, who art and
who wast, that thou hast taken thy great power and begun to
reign* (11:17). This song anticipates the arrival of the
kingdom of God at the end of time.

4. Before the kingdom can come, the chief spiritual
enemy of God and man has to be removed: *Now the
salvation and the power and the kingdom of our God and the
authority of his Christ have come, for the accuser of our breth-
ren (Satan) has been thrown down . . .* (12:10).

5. John also heard confirmed what he knew from
study of the Old Testament. The heavenly choir sang:
Great and wonderful are thy deeds, O Lord God the Almighty!

Just and true are thy ways, O King of the ages! (15:3). Later he heard the chorus: *Hallelujah! For the Lord our God the Almighty reigns* (19:6).

6. He also heard how God would achieve his universal rule. Jesus Christ will overcome all worldly powers who assist the cause of Satan: *They will make war on the Lamb, and the Lamb will conquer them, for he is Lord of lords and King of kings* (17:14). As a great warrior-king on a white horse, he will conquer: *On his robe and on his thigh he has a name inscribed, King of kings and Lord of lords* (19:16).

So we find that John is inspired to present the rule of the Lord Jesus as being the means or rule by which the everlasting LORD achieves the victory over all enemies and establishes the final, eternal kingdom. While the imagery is different, the doctrine is much the same as that of Paul.

One aspect of John's presentation of the victory of the exalted Jesus is the sharing with him in his rule and victory by his "saints" (see, e.g., 12:10 and 17:14), who are represented as a "kingdom" in whom he rules (1:6 and 5:10). The sharing by the saints in his reign is clearly stated in Revelation 20:4, 6; but the meaning of the "thousand years" of their reign is not clear. It seems best to take it to refer to the period from the exaltation of Christ until his return to earth in glory.*

SUMMARY

For Jesus, the kingdom of God was absolutely central. For the apostles, Jesus (the exalted Messiah and Lord)

---

*Perhaps some readers who are familiar with the Nicene Creed will feel that I have departed from its teaching when it declares: "He shall come again with glory to judge both the living and the dead: *whose kingdom shall have no end.*" The last six words appear to clash not only with what is written above, but also with Paul's words in 1 Corinthians 15:24, "Then comes the end, when he was absolutely central. Yet their messages are one. How? Because Jesus not only proclaimed the kingdom, he also embodied it. By the Holy Spirit—the Paraclete (= Counselor, Comforter, etc.)—Jesus, who embodies the kingdom, is proclaimed and obeyed in the Church. In Jesus, the exalted Lord made known by the Spirit, the kingdom is a present reality to the believing sinner.

The only way that the apostles could preach the kingdom was to preach the One who embodied the kingdom and who had defeated the kingdom of Satan, death, and hell.

QUESTIONS FOR DISCUSSION

1. What is the best way to explain and preach the Lordship of Jesus today so that it is meaningful to modern people?
2. If we say that there is a development of doctrine from the teaching of Jesus to that of the apostles, what precisely do we mean?

---

delivers the kingdom to God the Father after destroying every rule and every authority and power."

The answer to this apparent discrepancy is as follows. The clause in question was inserted by the bishops at the Council of Constantinople (381) as they revised the original creed of Nicaea (325). They wished to exclude the heresy of Marcellus, bishop of Ancyra. He taught that the son of God and the Holy Spirit did not exist within the eternal Godhead, but emerged from within the Godhead for the purposes of creation and redemption. These purposes completed, they would have no further independent existence. Therefore, in proclaiming that the Son of God is eternal and as such will forever have a people united to him, the bishops were by implication refuting the teaching of Marcellus. So we are to understand this clause as speaking of the eternal existence of the Son of God as one of the Three Persons of the Holy Trinity of the One God. The kingdom of God of the future will belong to the One God and thus to each of the Three Persons. The present kingdom of the Mediator, the Incarnate Son, will have been taken into the fullness of the kingdom of God.

4 SUMMARY

Before beginning the task of asking how the kingdom of God is related to the church, ethics, human society, and the future, a summary of the main points which have emerged will, I believe, be helpful and assist the task before us.

One real problem in using the word "kingdom" is that we tend automatically to think of a territory and if we constantly do this, especially in reading the Gospels, we shall often be confused! We need to remember that the word we translate "kingdom" has a flexible meaning in the original languages and can mean "reign," "realm," "rule," and "kingdom." The reason why "kingdom" is used most often in translations will become obvious as we proceed.

The kingdom of God is primarily a future reality. It is that state of affairs which will come into being at the end of this evil age, after the Last Judgment. Then God will not only be in control of everything, but everyone and everything will gladly acknowledge his rule. So this future kingdom is a realm, a sphere, and a rule. It was to this that the prophets looked forward, describing it in various ways, from "new heavens and earth" to "new Jerusalem." Jesus spoke of this as coming after his second coming. The kingdom of God will be the sphere in which, under the rule of God, believers enjoy the fullness of eternal salvation and in which their redemption is completed.

Because Jesus Christ is the Son of God in human flesh, his presence on earth meant that in him God's presence, rule, and peace, which belong essentially to the kingdom to come, are on earth. So he proclaimed that the kingdom has drawn near. In him, the future kingdom was a reality in the present. In him, the glory of the age to come was present on earth. God's kingdom was a reality in him not only because he is the eternal Son of God, but also because he lived in perfect communion with the Father and in perfect obedience to the Father. Therefore, to believe in him and to belong to him meant to be under the influence of the kingdom of God, or in other words, to be receiving God's salvation here and now.

In Paul's terms, the future kingdom is a reality in the present and is known to be so through the presence of the Holy Spirit in the heart. Not only does he whisper "You are God's child" (Romans 8:15) to the believer, but his presence is like a down payment, seal, and guarantee of the glorious fullness of the kingdom to come.

The kingdom was present in Jesus, and from him salvation came. But how is the kingdom present now, when he is seated as Lord at the right hand of the Father? The answer is straightforward. By his death and exaltation to heaven, Jesus conquered all the enemies of God and man—sin, Satan, and death. From heaven, the Father sent the Spirit to earth in order that in and by the Spirit the presence of Jesus himself could be known all over the world. So the kingdom of God becomes a reality in the lives of believers now through the presence of the indwelling Spirit (see Romans 14:17). Through the Spirit, they come into living contact with the exalted Lord Jesus and thus with the future kingdom; in him is the future salvation. Therefore, on this earth and in this life the kingdom of God is primarily the rule of God in human lives through the salvation which is given to them in the Spirit from the Lord Jesus. In their response of obedience and faith, they reveal that they are under the rule of God. And as they are ruled by God, they look forward with hope to that future wherein the whole order of reality will be perfect. They pray, "Your kingdom come. . . ."

How does the presence and rule of God with and over Israel in the covenant relationship fit into what we have been saying? Is that rule to be thought of as an anticipation of the future kingdom of God which will come at the end of the age? Or is it to be understood as a particular and special part of that sovereign (secret) rule of God over the world in this age? The answer, I think, is that it is both an anticipation of the kingdom of God to come and a special part of God's providential rule of the world in this age.

Both the Old and New Testaments make clear that the LORD is the Ruler of the whole cosmos and all within it. What theologians call the doctrine of providence is the study of God's rule of the universe. We know that not all human beings recognize this rule and that it has to be exercised against the presence and power of sin and Satan in the world. Much of God's rule in this present age is without the cooperation of his creatures, and thus it is very difficult to detect as a part of the history of nations, peoples, and tribes, unless the people be the Israelites. We affirm God is LORD of lords and King of kings by faith on the basis of scriptural teaching.

Since Israel was a nation among other nations, God's rule over this people was a part of his rule over all the nations in the world; the faithful Israelites, at least, recognized this. But in that the covenant relation was a relationship of unmerited favor, grace, mercy, and love from the Lord to Israel, and in that God's presence was experienced from time to time by the people, then in these the future kingdom of God was anticipated. The Israelites not only knew the Lord as the universal King, but they knew him as covenant LORD; and in these two types of experience of God, they knew that he was in control of this age and would be even more obviously in control of the age to come, for in that age all would gladly confess his kingship.

Therefore, we see why the expression "kingdom of God" is most used. The true kingdom, the fullness of the kingdom at the end of the age, is more than a rule by God; it is the realm and sphere also in which God's rule is known. In this age where the sphere is a fallen imperfect earth, the kingdom of God is the rule of God or the reign of grace in believing and obedient hearts, which is a foretaste of the fullness to come.

QUESTIONS FOR DISCUSSION

1. How can we help Christians to gain a clearer understanding of the richness of the biblical idea of the kingdom?

2. What is the difference between the rule of God over this present evil age and the rule of God in the kingdom to come?

PART II   APPLICATION

5 THE KINGDOM AND THE CHURCH

It is common in intercessory prayers to ask God to extend his kingdom through evangelistic work. Further, the phrase (or its equivalents) "working for the kingdom of God" is often used by believers to describe their Christian activity. So the question arises for the thoughtful person, "What is the relation of the church (of which Christians are members) and the kingdom (that is, the saving rule of God)?" Or, put another way, "Since the church is the church *of God* (1 Corinthians 1:2) and the kingdom is the kingdom *of God,* are the two phrases merely synonymous, referring to the same basic reality?" The answer is, as we shall see from the teaching of Jesus and of Paul, that while the two are intimately related, they are not synonymous; they must be distinguished in our thinking in order to have a clear understanding of God's activity in the world. In fact, as we shall also see, the church is the fellowship, community, or congregation in which the rule of God should be known and celebrated.

KINGDOM AND CHURCH: HOW RELATED?

First of all, we need to recognize that Jesus attempted to persuade the Jews of his day to receive the kingdom of God which had drawn near to them. The Gospel of Matthew makes this abundantly clear. Jesus sent the twelve apostles to preach only to "the lost sheep of the house of Israel" the message that "the kingdom of heaven is at hand" and to heal only Jewish sickness (10:5ff.). To all Jews who wanted fullness of life he said, "Come to me, all who labor and are heavy laden, and I will give you rest. Take my yoke upon you, and learn from me; for I am gentle and lowly in heart, and you will find rest for your souls. For my yoke is easy, and my burden is light" (11:28-30). When he met a Canaanite woman in the north of Palestine, he promptly told her when she asked for help, "I was sent only to the lost sheep of the house of Israel" (15:24).

What Jesus wanted was for the whole of Jewry to repent and, as little children, to receive the saving rule of God in their lives. When he realized that the Jews as a people would not receive his message and the gift of God's grace, he knew he had to create a new people for God, a new Israel, a new church, and to do it from the nucleus of believing, obedient Jews who received the kingdom.

The word "church" (Greek *ekklesia*), which is common in the Greek translation of the Old Testament as a description of the congregation of Israel, occurs only twice in the recorded teaching of Jesus, in Matthew 16:18, 19 and Matthew 18:17. Matthew 16:18, 19 contains the response of Jesus to the confession of Peter that Jesus was the Messiah. The recognition of his messiahship had to precede membership in the church.

Jesus said, "And I tell you, you are Peter *(petros)*, and

on this rock *(petra)* I will build my church, and the powers of death shall not prevail against it. I will give you
the keys of the kingdom of heaven, and whatever you
bind on earth shall be bound in heaven, and whatever
you loose on earth shall be loosed in heaven." One problem here is the identity of the rock, *petra.* If we follow
the best modern exegesis and take this rock to refer
primarily to Peter, the apostolic leader who confesses
the truth about Jesus (that he is Messiah), then that
problem is solved.

The problem which particularly concerns us is the
relation of the church and kingdom. Jesus said he would
build the church and give the keys of the kingdom to
Peter. A simple, but not satisfactory explanation is to say
that church and kingdom are equivalents on the basis
that Peter is given (to use picture language) the keys to
lock or unlock the house (the house being the church) or
the kingdom (the kingdom being where God rules).

A less simple, but a more satisfactory explanation is
the following. Jesus is presenting a picture of a royal
household in which the keys to all the important rooms
are held by the chief steward. These keys were given to
him by the king or emperor. The Messiah, Jesus himself, is the "chief steward" in the Father's rule and reign
in the world. Here, in anticipation of his future death
and resurrection (to which he refers in vv. 21ff.) and
ascension, he is giving to Peter, the leader and representative of the apostles, the position of chief steward. Later
Jesus committed this responsibility of stewardship to all
the apostles (see Matthew 18:18 and John 20:20-23).
They exercised it in their mission to the world.

The truth conveyed by this picture is that the apostles,
and Peter in particular, will have definite authority from
God; and this authority, being from God himself, will be

a part of the actual rule and salvation of God in human lives.

As Jesus had interpreted and fulfilled the law of God given through Moses (Matthew 5), so now authority is given to the apostles to interpret this law (as did Peter in Acts 10:44ff. in the case of Gentiles) and to exercise discipline (as did Peter in the case of Ananias and Sapphira in Acts 5, and as did Paul in the case of the Corinthians—1 Corinthians 5:4, 5, etc.). In these actions of applying God's Word, and thus God's rule, they would be working only as unworthy servants, but nevertheless—by God's grace—as faithful servants.

This explanation is in harmony with the meaning of the expression "to bind and to loose." It was in common use by the rabbis at the time and meant the permitting or forbidding of actions. Therefore, God would ratify the decisions of the apostles at the last judgment. Furthermore, this explanation is in harmony with the teaching of Paul that the church is built upon Christ, the chief cornerstone, and on the apostles as secondary foundation stones (Ephesians 2:20).

Therefore, what we learn from Matthew 16:18, 19 is that Jesus Christ builds the church, which is the community of his disciples, through the work of his apostles and their successors. As the servants of Christ and of God and as his stewards, the apostles are given the authority in the power of the Spirit (as Acts and Paul's letters make clear) to be the means and instruments of God's saving rule. They function in this way in the churches, the community of those who have submitted to God's rule and salvation, by the way they interpret the Word of God and the way they exercise discipline.

It may be asked, What is the relation of the authority/discipline of the kingdom of God to local churches today? The beginnings of the answer to this question lie, I believe, in the right understanding of the words of Jesus recorded in Matthew 18:18-20. This section immediately follows his teaching on discipline within the local congregation of disciples of the kingdom. Jesus said, "Truly, I say to you, whatever you bind on earth shall be bound in heaven and whatever you loose on earth shall be loosed in heaven. Again I say to you, if two of you agree on earth about anything they ask, it will be done for them by my Father in heaven. For where two or three are gathered in my name, there am I in the midst of them."

Here it is promised that Christ himself is acting within his churches through the membership in such matters of discipline as are outlined in verses 15-17. Thus, "to bind and to loose" is not a unique, apostolic duty or privilege. What is a unique, apostolic activity is laying a foundation (which the apostles did) as stewards of the kingdom of God—they founded churches and wrote the New Testament. But in the day to day implementation of the discipline and authority of the rule of God in the church congregation, churches have within themselves already the appropriate means under Christ the King "to bind and to loose."

Paul is clear that the kingdom of God is not the church. He pictures Jesus Christ as the exalted Lord ruling the people of God through the Spirit. By the Spirit, through the proclamation of the gospel by his disciples, Christ calls people to respond to God's initiative of grace. By the same Spirit, the presence of Christ is with the disciples as they meet in worship and fellowship, and there are spiritual gifts to edify the church. Christ builds the church by the Spirit. For Paul, the kingdom is not the church, but is the action and rule of

God which builds and sustains the church. To be in the
kingdom is to be set free from the evil powers of the
universe and to have salvation: "God has delivered us
from the dominion of darkness and transferred us to
the kingdom of his beloved Son, in whom we have redemption, the forgiveness of sins" (Colossians 1:13).
Therefore, the church is the company of those who
have been released from Satan's power and have salvation; that is, they taste the powers of the age to come
(Hebrews 6:5), and are the first fruits of the new creation (James 1:18).

On the basis of this distinction between the kingdom
and church, it is now possible to make three further
points concerning their relationship. First of all, it needs
always to be remembered that the kingdom is always
prior to the church. God is King; as King he has a kingdom (reign or rule of grace) and offers the gift of salvation in and through the Messiah. Because the kingdom
exists in and through Christ, people repent and believe
the gospel, submitting to the rule of God and receiving
the gift of forgiveness. The kingdom came in Jesus
Christ, and he then created the church. Jesus preached
the gospel of the kingdom before he called the apostles
and disciples together to form the nucleus of the new-
covenant people of God. Paul taught that the whole initiative in the salvation of mankind was from God, for
God was in Christ reconciling the world to himself (2
Corinthians 5:19). He also made clear that the origin of
the rule of God in the human heart and its continuance
there was the work of the Spirit (Romans 8:5 ff.) So
God's initiative and rule is always prior to the creation of
churches composed of believing and repentant sinners.

Secondly, it is clear from the teaching of Jesus that his
disciples were to be heralds of and witnesses to the

kingdom. They were to tell what they had seen (mighty works defeating Satan and his kingdom) and heard (the gospel, from Jesus, of the saving rule of God). When Jesus sent out the twelve (Matthew 10:1ff.; Mark 6:7ff.; Luke 9:1-6) and the seventy (Luke 10:1-24) on their missions, he sent them as witnesses of the kingdom as well as his assistants. They were an extension of his own ministry, and thus he gave to them the "power of the kingdom." Later, as the resurrected Messiah soon to be enthroned at the right hand of the Father, he sent his disciples into the whole world from Jerusalem, through Judea and Samaria, to the far corners of the earth (Acts 1:8). And he sent them with a gospel, the good news of the gracious rule of God which had drawn near in himself, as Messiah and Lord, bringing the gift of salvation to the world.

Witnesses do more than merely speak what they know to be true. They live by what they know to be true. So disciples witnessed to the kingdom, said Jesus, by how they lived. For example, he emphasized the grace of humility and a forgiving spirit as signs of being under the rule of God and enjoying his salvation (see Mark 10:35-45; Matthew 6:12-14; 18:23-35). Proclaiming God's rule and living under it belong together as the privilege and duty of believers.

Paul wholeheartedly believed that the Church is to witness to God's kingdom; that is, to God's provision in Jesus Christ of salvation for the world. By example (think of his journeys) and by teaching (think of the Letters), he encouraged both true evangelism in the Roman Empire and a style of life in pagan society worthy of the name of Jesus the Lord. Not that he believed that the Church itself could bring in or extend the kingdom (for God alone rules and can rule), but that

witnessing and working were the proper activities of
those in whom God ruled. In this sense, he could call
several friends "fellow workers for the kingdom of God"
(Colossians 4:11).

Thirdly, the Church as the servant of God opposes
the kingdom of Satan (evil) in the name of Christ. In
human affairs, the kingdom of evil works to initiate and
maintain such modern realities as injustice, discrimination, atheism, sensualism, poverty, pursuit of the occult,
and materialistic values. These have to be attacked in
the name of the Lord Jesus, for in him "God disarmed
the principalities and powers and made a public example of them, triumphing over them" (Colossians 2:15).
The people of God cannot stand aside and watch evil
grow, but rather by appropriate means (e.g., the sword
of the Spirit = Word of God, prayer, and loving service)
are to participate in the spiritual war, knowing that they
are on the victory side.

In the next two chapters this theme of witnessing and
service will be developed and applied to contemporary
life.

To summarize: The kingdom of God and the church
of God are two different concepts. The first is the gracious rule of the Father through the Son in the power of
the Holy Spirit, providing salvation in the reign of grace
for individual sinners who repent and believe. The second is the result of this rule in terms of the creation of a
people who live under the saving rule of God. Therefore, he who is in the kingdom (in whom rules Christ by
the Spirit) is normally in a church, but there could be
circumstances in which a disciple of the kingdom was
not a church member (e.g., if he resided on a desert
island). The kingdom is always prior to the church, and
the church properly functions when it is a witness to the

kingdom. Yet it must not be forgotten that the church is a divine creation and so not to be equated with any other type of human society. (I have developed this thought in my book, *God's Church Today*.)

CELEBRATING THE KINGDOM OF GOD IN CHURCH WORSHIP

Here I want to present the idea that the kingdom of God is primarily experienced by the contemporary church in the service of corporate worship. God's rule, his reign of grace, is so important an element in true worship that corporate worship may be called the celebration of the kingdom of God. In our society we celebrate birthdays, anniversaries, successes of various kinds, victory at war and in sports or politics, and other events with appropriate ritual, ceremony, and festivity. In worship as the people of God, we celebrate, proclaim, and rejoice in the fact that God's kingdom and thus his salvation has drawn near to us in Jesus Christ, and that God's kingdom and salvation are here now in the presence and power of the Holy Spirit.

Before becoming more specific in terms of the worship of the people of the new covenant, let us remind ourselves that the Israelites of the old covenant celebrated the kingship of God in their worship. This is clear from such Psalms as 47, 93, 96, 97, 98, and 99. When these are read aloud, the feeling of celebration which was present at the festivals in the Temple becomes clear. Here are two examples:

Ascribe to the Lord, you families of nations,
ascribe to the Lord glory and might;
ascribe to the Lord the glory due to his name,
bring a gift and come into his courts.
Bow down to the Lord in the splendour of holiness,

and dance in his honour, all men on earth.
Declare among the nations, "The Lord is king.
He has fixed the earth firm, immovable;
he will judge the peoples justly."

(96:7-10, NEB)

The Lord is king, let the earth be glad,
let coasts and islands all rejoice.

(97:1, NEB)

Two themes are apparent in these psalms of celebration. The LORD is proclaimed as the King of the universe, and nations who do not know the LORD are called upon to recognize this King. Then the LORD is proclaimed as the King of Israel, the One who made the covenant at Sinai and the One who exercises his kingship in terms of saving acts and covenant faithfulness. He comes to visit his people. So God is celebrated as the King who constantly watches over Israel and who sometimes draws near in saving acts to bless or rescue Israel. While there are definite signs of his presence and rule—e.g., the ark of the covenant—his rule is essentially exercised, as it were, from outside, for he is not permanently present with Israel.

If the Israelites had cause to celebrate, how much more have Christians! They celebrate that the LORD is King, the King of kings and Lord of lords (Revelation 17:14); he is the universal ruler, a fact which remains true even if the nations do not yet acknowledge or recognize his rule. He is the Lord of history, the One who guides the fortunes of nations and individuals. They also celebrate God's kingship exercised in and on behalf of Israel, for the record of this relationship is a part of the history of God's salvation recorded in Holy Scripture.

Preeminently they celebrate the rule of God which came in Jesus Christ. In and through Jesus, the kingdom of God—the gracious, saving rule of God—was permanently on earth, since where Jesus was there was the kingdom. Through his victory over sin, death, hell, and Satan, which he achieved on the Cross and in resurrection and ascension, and through his sending from the Father the Holy Spirit to be his Representative in the world, the kingdom of God is now universal. Wherever the Holy Spirit brings God's salvation and rule to penitent hearts and wherever those in whom God rules meet together, then there is the kingdom of God. What the physical eye sees is people living new lives; but what the eye of faith sees is the presence of God, the rule of God, the grace of God in their hearts.

Therefore, when a church assembles for worship, it assembles as a people in whom God dwells and to whom God has given the gift of forgiveness and salvation. To celebrate the kingdom of God is to praise God for Jesus Christ, whose life was lived wholly in the kingdom of God, totally under God's control. It is to praise God for the victory which Christ won over sin and death in his resurrection and ascension. It is to rejoice in the experience now of the presence of Christ by the Holy Spirit in the hearts and the fellowship of the church members. It is to have the assurance of God's salvation now, a salvation which will be brought to completion at the end of the age in the fullness of the universal kingdom of God. And it is to watch and pray, knowing that this age will not end before the Lord Jesus returns in glory to judge the nations and complete his work as Messiah and Lord.

To celebrate the kingdom is to celebrate God as the King not only of nature, but also of grace and salvation. The positive side of celebration is praise, thanksgiving, and rejoicing, for there is truly much to be excited about in God's kingdom. The negative side is self-examination, penitence, and confession for failure to allow God to rule as he wishes in our lives.

Celebration should be a prominent part of all types of corporate worship, be they liturgical or extemporary. However, it is particularly prominent in the service we call the Lord's Supper or Eucharist, which was instituted by our Lord himself (Matthew 26:20ff.; Mark 14:17ff.; Luke 22:14ff.; 1 Corinthians 11:23ff.). This service focuses not only on the atoning sacrificial death of Jesus, but also on his ascension into heaven and his future coming in glory at the end of the age. Without the incarnate Son of God defeating the powers of evil in our universe, there would have been no rule of God in our lives and no gift of forgiveness. So this service celebrates the kingdom of God in Jesus Christ. One modern service for the Lord's Supper has the following lines in it which express the theme of what I am saying. It is the *Service of Holy Communion* (1973), produced by the Church of England in Australia.

Therefore, Father, with this bread and this cup
we proclaim his perfect sacrifice
made once for all upon the cross;
we celebrate the redemption he has won for us;
and we look for his coming
to fulfill all things according to your will.

And,

Grant that we who eat and drink these holy things
may be filled with your life and goodness for ever.
Renew us by your holy Spirit,
that we may be united in the body of your Son
and be brought with all your people

into the joy of your eternal kingdom;
through Jesus Christ our Lord,
with whom and in whom,
by the power of the Holy Spirit,
we worship you, Father Almighty,
in never-ending praise:
Blessing and honour and glory and power
are yours for ever and ever. *Amen.*

To participate in the Lord's Supper on Sunday is particularly appropriate since the Lord's Day is the day of the Resurrection, the day when death and sin were defeated.

Celebration in worship is that which prepares the church for its mission in the world. Therefore, the service quoted above ends with this prayer:

Father, we offer ourselves to you
in Jesus Christ our Lord.
Send us out in the power of your Spirit
to live and work to your praise and glory.

So Christians are witnesses of God's kingdom, a simple but yet a profound calling.

QUESTIONS FOR DISCUSSION

1. What would be the implications if the kingdom of God and the church of God were the same reality?
2. Does the idea of worship as celebration help to increase your understanding of, or desire for, corporate worship?

6   THE KINGDOM AND ETHICS

The principles which should govern human behavior are much discussed today in all walks of life and among all age groups. Much heat is generated by ethical problems—abortion, homosexuality, euthanasia, etc.—because people begin from different premises, as wide-ranging as protecting the status quo to the need for total revolution. When of sober mind, we all accept that ethics cannot exist unless there are some foundations from which we construct our principles of behavior; these foundations may be implicitly or explicitly held.

Christians are under the rule of God; they are citizens of the kingdom of God. Therefore, their ethics must be determined by their membership of the kingdom, for this is the most important reality in their lives. To adopt any other position or to begin from any other basis is to deny their Lord. Yet even Christians disagree on ethical matters. Why? There are at least two basic reasons. First of all, to arrive at Christian ethical principles you have to understand the teaching of the Bible, and in many cases this is not an easy task. We are separated by nearly 2,000 years from the time of the apostles, and we cannot always easily enter into their minds to know what they or earlier writers intended. Secondly, the situation in which Christian ethical principles are to be applied is, to say the least, complex. Human society in the time of Jesus and Paul was, relatively speaking, simple in comparison with our technological, scientifically-based society. Many of our acute moral dilemmas of today are related to the "progress" we enjoy through scientific discovery and technological advance.

We shall look first at the teaching of Jesus and then of Paul concerning the relation of the kingdom of God and personal ethics. In a brief conclusion, I shall attempt to relate what we have ascertained to our life in the modern world. Then I shall turn in the next chapter to the problem of the relation of the kingdom of God to social ethics.

THE TEACHING OF JESUS

We turn first to the Sermon on the Mount (Matthew 5–7), where Jesus speaks of the kingdom eight times. Of these, some point to the rule of God which brings salvation and is experienced here and now (e.g., 5:3, 10), while others refer to the kingdom to come (e.g., 7:21). One paragraph from the Sermon specifically brings together the kingdom and ethics. It is 5:17-20:

Think not that I have come to abolish the law and the prophets; I have come not to abolish them but to fulfil them. For truly, I say to you, till heaven and earth pass away, not an iota, not a dot, will pass from the law until all is accomplished. Whoever then relaxes one of the least of these commandments and teaches men so, shall be called least in the kingdom of heaven; but he who does them and teaches them shall be called great in the kingdom of heaven. For I tell you, unless your righteousness exceeds that of the scribes and Pharisees, you will never enter the kingdom of heaven.

This is not an easy passage to interpret, but we must

make the effort. It appears that in his teaching Jesus is
stating a positive position against two false positions. On
the one hand, there is the teaching of the Pharisees who
tended to miss the real demands of the law of God by
their sophisticated explanations and developments of it;
on the other, there is the teaching of those (who became
common in the churches and said, "let us sin that grace
may abound") who took Christian freedom to mean
exemption from obedience to God's law.

However, from this passage we see Jesus claiming
that:

1. He established the contents of the Law (= Torah,
the first five books of the Bible) and the Prophets (from
Samuel to Malachi) by realizing and actualizing them
both in his personal life and in his teaching. He obeyed
the Law of Moses as God intended and fulfilled the
prophecies concerning the Messiah. As the kingdom
was present in him and his ministry, so the ethics of the
kingdom were realized in his thoughts, attitudes, and
behavior.

2. Until the end of the age, the Old Testament remains God's Word. (The "iota" and the "dot" are the
smallest letters of the Greek and Hebrew alphabets.
Thus, verse 18 is a dramatic way of emphasizing the
permanence of God's Word until the kingdom comes in
its fullness at the end of time. Yet, as Matthew 5:21ff.
makes clear, it is God's Word interpreted by God's Messiah.)

3. To make distinctions (as did certain rabbis) between important ("heavy") and unimportant ("light")
commands in God's Torah in order only to obey the
important ones is not acceptable to God. (To be "least"
or "great" in the kingdom means to be reckoned by God
himself as such. The "greatest" is the servant of all—see
Matthew 20:25-27.)

4. Since the scribes (lawyers) and Pharisees missed the real meaning of the Torah and reflected this in their life-styles, the lives of disciples of the kingdom must be morally and spiritually superior, showing that they understand the meaning of the Torah and truly live under the rule of God.

Jesus explained the way to understand the Law of Moses in verses 21-48, which are the best commentary on verses 17-20 that we could ever have. Here we find six antitheses in which Jesus challenged the interpretation of the Law by the Pharisees. What Jesus was in fact doing was interpreting God's commands in a higher key, intensifying them and bringing out their fullest or ultimate meaning.

Thus, when he spoke of the command not to murder, he interpreted it as covering not only the outward act of murder, but that anger in the heart which precedes actual murder and that insulting word or attitude which is aimed at character assassination. The way of the disciple of the kingdom is not anger, insult, or murder, but reconciliation (verses 21-26). In a similar manner, when he spoke of adultery he saw the command of God as forbidding not only the outward physical act, but also that inner desire for sexual intercourse with a member of the opposite sex which is called lust (verses 27-30). Finally, we may note that he interpreted loving the neighbor not as requiring the hating of the enemy (as did some Pharisees), but as loving the enemy and praying for persecutors (verses 43-48).

The basis of these ethics is love. But not just any kind of love! It is, rather, the love which was displayed by the heavenly Father in sending his Son into the world (John 3:16) and by the Son in loving those who did not love him. In Mark 12:28-34, there is an account of the reply which Jesus gave to a Jewish lawyer who asked Jesus,

"Which commandment is the first of all?" Jesus an-
swered that there were in fact two, the first being to love
God with our whole being and the second to love others
as we love ourselves. Jesus claimed that the whole moral
law of God could be summed up under these two
duties—to love God and human beings.

However, when we ask ourselves, "How do we love
ourselves?" the answer, if we are honest, must be that we
love ourselves selfishly. We are sinners, and we tend
always to think of ourselves first. Therefore, since Jesus
knew that our hearts are imperfect, he made clear the
meaning of loving others by giving it definite content.
After washing the sweaty and dusty feet of his disciples
he said, "A new commandment I give to you, that you
love one another" (John 13:34). Later that day Jesus
referred to himself as the "true Vine" to whom his disciples ("branches") are united, and he said, "This is my
commandment, that you love one another as I have
loved you" (John 15:12). So to love the neighbor is to
imitate Christ; it is to love as he loved. Such an approach
lifts the life of the disciples above the mere keeping of
rules and regulations. It encourages an attitude toward
others which fulfills and surpasses the demands of the
moral law.

Several parables of Jesus also illustrate this point. In
that of the Good Samaritan (Luke 10:29-37), it is the
concern of the Samaritan for the man who is in great
need at the side of the road which illustrates what loving
the neighbor means. Then in the story of the rich man
(Dives) and Lazarus (Luke 16:19-31), the punishment of
the rich man is not because he had been deliberately
cruel to Lazarus, the poor beggar. The problem was that
he had not noticed the existence of the man in great
need at his own gate. Then in the story of the sheep and
goats (Matthew 25:31-46), the final judgment is based

not on what has been said or believed by the disciples, but rather on what has been done to care for those in need—widows, orphans, prisoners, etc.

So it is clear that at the root of the ethics of Jesus lies the demand for love in the heart, both in attitude and in action. In the way he lived in his relation to God and human beings, Jesus provided an example of his own ethics. In our Western society, love is used in so many ways, and most of them far removed from the biblical idea of love (Greek *agape*), that to appreciate what Jesus meant by love we have to study carefully both his life and teaching. Otherwise, we shall quite sincerely think that we are loving our neighbor when in fact we are only loving in the way which our society generally requires of us—which may be much less or rather different from what God requires.

Another way of expressing the call of Jesus for perfect love to God and man is to say that he made a call for radical obedience to and trust of God along with radical concern for the good of human beings. The disciple of the kingdom has to place allegiance to God above allegiance to either family or possessions. In the presence of his mother Jesus said, "Whoever does the will of God is my brother, and sister, and mother" (Mark 3:35). And in the Sermon on the Mount, he spoke of laying up treasure in heaven, not on earth—of serving God, not mammon (money), and seeking first and foremost the kingdom of God.

In radical concern for human beings, Jesus often explained the principle of loving the neighbor which we discussed above. In this context comes the famous Golden Rule: "Whatever you wish that men would do to you, do so to them; for this is the law and the prophets" (Matthew 7:12).

In the light of the perfectionist and radical nature of

the ethic of Jesus, it is often asked whether fulfillment is possible by disciples of the kingdom here on earth in this evil age. The answer must be negative. Of necessity, since his ethic is the demand and command of a righteous and holy Lord, it must be an absolute ethic, and as such only attainable by those who are totally free of sin and perfectly motivated toward God. However, as we know, no disciple of the kingdom is ever wholly free from sin. Thus, the ethic of Jesus functions as a challenge, as a mountain to be climbed and a goal to be reached. Failure is met with the Father's forgiving love (as the Lord's Prayer makes clear) and with the call of Jesus once more to be perfect as the heavenly Father is perfect. The absolute ethic demonstrates that the rule of God is the rule of the kingdom to come. Entry into the future kingdom is not a reward for trying to obey the ethic of Jesus. Rather, entry into the kingdom is the gift of God (Luke 12:32), yet a gift which must be exhibited by the disciples in terms of loving submission to the divine rule—which means following the ethic of Jesus.

God rules in the heart to a lesser or greater degree to the extent that the disciple responds to the grace and commands of his Lord and King. And it would appear that for those who respond with a full heart and mind and seek by God's help always to do his will, there are rewards in the future kingdom. Jesus refers to these in Matthew 6:1-18; 10:41ff.; 16:27; 18:23-35; Mark 9:41; 10:29-31; Luke 6:23, 32-35. These rewards flow from the richness of the grace of God, but the exact nature of them we do not know.

One final point needs to be made concerning the ethic of Jesus. It is this. To be committed to the ethic of Jesus is to be committed to him as a person. Jesus told the rich man not only to sell all he had and keep the commandments but also, "Come, follow me" (Mark 10:21). To his disciples, he called for commitment both to his words and his person: "If any man would come after me, let him deny himself and take up his cross and follow me . . ." (Mark 8:34-38).

THE TEACHING OF PAUL

When we listed the verses in Paul's Letters where he actually spoke specifically of the kingdom, we noted that a dominant theme in them was the ethical demand of God's rule. See, for example, 1 Corinthians 6:9-11, Galatians 5:19-21, and Ephesians 5:5. It was for Paul a matter of straightforward logic. God is the righteous Ruler who cannot demand anything less than righteousness from disciples of the kingdom. They are to "be imitators of God, as beloved children" (Ephesians 5:1), which reminds us of the command of Jesus that we are to be perfect as the heavenly Father is perfect. The demand for righteous and holy living as required by the character and will of God is a constant theme in Paul— see Romans 12:1ff.; 14:17; Ephesians 4:24; 5:10, 17; 6:6; Colossians 1:10; 4:12; 1 Thessalonians 2:12; 4:1-3.

Paul also emphasized the ethical demands of the kingdom of God through his doctrines of the Lordship of Christ and the kingdom of Christ, topics we examined in Chapter Three. He taught that all who repent and believe the gospel are united to Christ, by the Spirit, in his death, resurrection, and ascension. They live their Christian lives "in Christ." That is, from the divine standpoint they are seen as being in Christ and as such are forgiven, justified, and reconciled to God. Christ, the Lord, embodies and exemplifies the kingdom of God, and, being united to him in faith by the eternal Spirit, believers are in the kingdom of God. So God does not see their sinfulness, but he sees instead the perfect righteousness of Christ himself. For this teaching of

Paul, see Romans 6:1-14; 13:14; 1 Corinthians 11:1; 2
Corinthians 10:1-6; Galatians 2:20ff.; 3:27; 6:2; Ephesians 2:4-10; Philippians 1:10ff.; and Colossians 2:6.
From this position of being in Christ and thus certain
members of the future kingdom of God, Paul deduces
strong ethical implications. After emphasizing that believers died with Christ on the Cross and rose with him
from death (symbolically presented by baptism) Paul
stated, "So you must also consider yourselves dead to sin
and alive to God in Christ Jesus. Let not sin therefore
reign in your mortal bodies, to make you obey their
passions . . ." (Romans 6:11, 12). What we are in God's
sight in Christ, we are to become by the power of the
Spirit in reality. This is a call to perfection, which is a
goal toward which we move. Paul claimed, "I press on
toward the goal for the prize of the upward call of God
in Christ Jesus" (Philippians 3:14).

As the exalted Lord, Christ sends the Spirit as his
Representative in the world. By the help of the Spirit
(whose presence means the presence of the
kingdom—Romans 14:17), believers are to live under
the rule of God. This means walking or living in the
Spirit. Paul told the Galatians to "walk by the Spirit" and
not to gratify the desires of the old human nature. They
were to cultivate the fruit of the Spirit, which is "love,
joy, peace, patience, kindness, goodness, faithfulness,
gentleness, and self-control" (Galatians 5:16, 22). This
theme of living in the power of the Spirit to imitate the
pattern of life set by the Lord Jesus is developed by Paul
in Romans 8:1-14, 1 Corinthians 3:1ff., 11:1, and Ephesians 4:29.

Another way of expressing this life of living under the
Lordship of Christ by the Spirit and thus living under
the rule of God is to speak of walking in love, that love
which is produced in the heart by the presence of the

Spirit. Following the example and teaching of Jesus, Paul taught that "love does no wrong to a neighbor; therefore love is the fulfilling of the law" (Romans 13:10). To do harm to a weaker Christian is no longer to walk in love (Romans 14:15), for all that a Christian does should be motivated by love ("Let all that you do be done in love"—1 Corinthians 16:14). Nowhere does Paul make this clearer than in that hymn of love found in 1 Corinthians 13.

> Love is patient and kind; love is not jealous or boastful; it is not arrogant or rude. Love does not insist on its own way; it is not irritable or resentful; it does not rejoice at wrong, but rejoices in the right. Love bears all things, believes all things, hopes all things, endures all things.
>
> Love never ends; as for prophecies, they will pass away; as for tongues, they will cease; as for knowledge, it will pass away. For our knowledge is imperfect and our prophecy is imperfect; but when the perfect comes, the imperfect will pass away. When I was a child, I spoke like a child, I thought like a child, I reasoned like a child; when I became a man, I gave up childish ways. For now we see in a mirror dimly, but then face to face. Now I know in part; then I shall understand fully, even as I have been fully understood. So faith, hope, love abides, these three; but the greatest of these is love.

The love described here is, of course, an imitation of the love of God displayed in the Lord Jesus.

Paul's idea of love was not a sentimental one. He held that those who walked in the love of God would fulfill the moral law; they would not steal, murder, or commit adultery, and neither would they cherish evil thoughts in their hearts. To the Ephesian Christians he wrote, "And walk in love as Christ loved us and gave himself up for us, a fragrant offering and sacrifice to God" (5:2). Jesus fulfilled the Law by a life of love and by his sacrifice of himself on the Cross. To the Colossian Chris-

tians he wrote, "And above all these (e.g., kindness, low-
liness, meekness, and patience) put on love, which binds
everything together in perfect harmony" (3:14). Here
love is pictured as an outer garment keeping the inner
garments in place.

So strong was Paul's sense of doing God's will in this
life that he often spoke of the judgment at the end of
the age when everyone would give an account for his
deeds before entering the kingdom of God. He told the
Roman Christians that "we shall all stand before the
judgment seat of God" and "each of us shall give account of himself to God" (14:10-12). For further teaching on this theme, see 2 Corinthians 5:10; Galatians 6:5,
7; Ephesians 6:8; and Colossians 3:25.

Paul is often accused of having a very conservative (as
opposed to the modern "enlightened" or "liberal") approach to such basic social institutions as marriage, the
family, and slavery. This accusation is justified as far as
it goes; but it must be accompanied by the insistence that
as far as Christians were concerned, Paul placed these
institutions under the Lordship of Christ and in the
presence of the Holy Spirit. Therefore, while he accepted the subordination of the wife to the husband, he
affirmed their mutual interdependence in the Lord
Jesus (1 Corinthians 11:11, 12). Also, he gave the example of the love of Christ for the church as that which the
husband should imitate in his love for his wife (Ephesians 5:21ff.).

With respect to household slavery, it is true that Paul
never challenged it as a legal institution. However, a
careful reading of the Letter to Philemon makes clear
that he expected "revolutionary" attitudes from both
Christian slaves and masters. Onesimus, the slave, was to
be a "beloved brother" of Philemon, the master. Exactly
why Paul never seems to have challenged the institution

of slavery we do not know. Perhaps he believed that the transforming power of Christ would change this institution from within and begin a gentle revolution within society; or perhaps he believed that since "the form of this world is passing away" (1 Corinthians 7:31), there were more important things to be getting on with.

CONCLUSION

The ethics of the kingdom of God are the principles of behavior to which Christians aspire. Since they demand purity of heart, they cannot be made into the law of a country; and since they require love in the heart (a part of us hidden from others), they cannot even become the rules for ordering the community life of a church. The rules by which a congregation orders its life will certainly be more demanding spiritually and morally than the laws of a country, but they will only be a part of the total ethics of the kingdom. For example, a church member can be disciplined for committing adultery, but not for lust.

Living as a disciple of Jesus Christ in modern Western, technological society is a tremendous challenge. The application of the absolute ethics of the kingdom to the complexities of contemporary life and culture is an exacting and sometimes exhausting enterprise. The reign of God challenges us in every area of life—e.g., how we build houses and live in them, use natural resources, employ technological products, eat and waste food, wear clothing, spend money, pursue education, relate to the poor and underprivileged, and help any in need.

The tendency of young Christians is to rebel against the seeming capitulation of older Christians to the standards of the consumer society, while the tendency of older Christians is to find good reasons for accepting many of the values and much of the produce of this society. Each of us must seek to analyze our motivation at any particular period in life. Christians have a duty to immerse their minds in the teaching of Scripture, and then use every means available to understand it and apply it to the real concrete situations in which they live. In the last analysis, all moral decisions are intensely personal, and thus the priority of conscience must be affirmed and maintained. However, what instructs the conscience is of great importance. So apart from using good aids to ascertain the precise meaning of Scripture, we need to use all the resources available—discussion with other Christians, books on ethical issues, study of society to ascertain its built-in standards and aims in order to make (hopefully by the guidance of the Holy Spirit) the right decisions followed by the appropriate action and life-style.

Those who are in positions of leadership in the churches—from Sunday school teachers to pastors, theologians, and professors—have a special responsibility to seek to achieve clarity of mind concerning the way in which the ethics of the kingdom are applicable at the personal and church fellowship level. For not only do they need to inform their own consciences concerning what God's rule requires; they also will be asked to help to inform the consciences of others in their roles as teachers and counselors.

QUESTIONS FOR DISCUSSION

1. If the ethics of the kingdom are absolute, what is the purpose in seeking to achieve them?
2. At what points does the ethic of Jesus most obviously challenge the life-style of the average Western Christian?

7 THE KINGDOM AND SOCIETY

Here we face what is probably the most difficult task in
this book, the attempt to relate the biblical idea of the
kingdom to human society as we know it today in the
"three worlds." In this task, the temptation is always to
start with an aspect of this world—e.g., poverty, oppression, affluence, the tensions in the Middle East or between the Communist and Western worlds—and then
seek to make the biblical doctrine fit into, or agree with,
our analysis of a given problem. For example, many
sincere "conservative" Christians fall into the trap of
overemphasizing the role of the State of Israel in God's
rule of the world today, while many sincere "liberal"
Christians fuse God's plans with those of socialist re-
formers or Marxist revolutionaries.

Conscious that I am walking into an area which either
has not been carefully explored or in which there is little
agreement, I shall look at the following topics. First, I
shall seek to present the doctrine of God's rule as King
over the world and its history. Secondly, I shall present
the kingdom of God as the goal of mission. And thirdly,
I shall make suggestions concerning the relationship of

the kingdom of God to social, political, and economic
concerns of today.

KING OF THE NATIONS

Under the threat of invasion from one or other of the
great empires of the ancient Near East or of war with
one or other of the small adjoining states, the faithful
Israelite trusted in the LORD as the King of the nations.
He or she affirmed, "I lift up my eyes to the hills. From
whence does my help come? My help comes from the
LORD, who made heaven and earth." And, "The Lord
will keep your going out and coming in from this time
forth and for evermore" (Psalm 121:1, 8). Also, Israelites looked to the LORD as the invisible Ruler over their
own history as a people and knew that God acted on
their behalf, both in blessing and in judgment (Psalm
91:1-7; Deuteronomy 8:3).

In a similar manner, the modern Christian, faced with
the barrage of news items from all over the world, trusts
in the LORD as the Ruler over all. He knows that it was
in God's appointed time that the eternal Son became
man: "When the time had fully come, God sent forth his
Son . . ." (Galatians 4:4). And with the redeemed in
heaven he rejoices that "the Lord our God the Almighty
reigns" (Revelation 19:6).

God is controlling the history of the nations, and he
will close history at his appointed time. This is the faith
of the Bible, but it is a faith which cannot be adequately
explained since the evidence is richly complex and is
wholly known only by God himself. Therefore, in the
Bible *God's rule is presented as being beyond human understanding.* Through Isaiah the LORD said, "My thoughts
are not your thoughts, neither are your ways my ways"
(55:8). Having meditated on the Lord's rule in history

Paul exclaimed, "O the depth of the riches and wisdom and knowledge of God! How unsearchable are his judgments and how inscrutable his ways!" (Romans 11:33). The inspired psalmist, thinking of the great deliverance from Egypt, a supreme example of God's rule, sang, "Thy way was through the sea, thy path through the great waters; yet thy footprints were unseen" (Psalm 77:19). Here, by a simple picture of footsteps the mystery involved in God's activity is presented.

Secondly, *God's rule is presented as being incapable of being ultimately thwarted, overcome, or subdued.* His "throne is established from of old" and "his decrees are very sure" (Psalm 93:2, 5). Yet, as Isaiah 53 and the New Testament make clear, the invincibility of the Lord is achieved in a way that involves the humiliation of the eternal Son of God (see Luke 24:26; Acts 2:23; 4:27, 28). Divine victory is not achieved by overcoming weak opponents, but by suffering with and for them.

Thirdly, *God's rule is usually presented without respect to what moderns call primary and secondary causes.* Job saw God's activity as directly affecting his life, even though he was aware of definite Satanic and human factors. He said:

Thy hands fashioned and made me;
and now thou dost turn about and destroy me.
Remember that thou hast made me of clay;
and wilt thou turn me to dust again?
Didst thou not pour me out like milk
and curdle me like cheese?

(10:8-10)

Likewise, the psalmist saw changes in nature as being caused directly by God:

The voice of the LORD breaks the cedars,

The LORD breaks the cedars of Lebanon.
He makes Lebanon to skip like a calf,
and Sirion like a young wild ox.

(Psalm 29:5, 6)

Further, we note that events in history were seen as being directly traceable to God. Here are some statements from the book of Proverbs:

A man's mind plans his way,
but the LORD directs his steps.

(16:9)

The king's heart is a stream of water in the hand of the LORD; he turns it wherever he will.

(21:1)

No wisdom, no understanding, no counsel,
can avail against the LORD.
The horse is made ready for the day of battle,
but the victory belongs to the LORD.

(21:30, 31)

The song of Moses in Exodus 15 is a full illustration of this conviction that the Lord rules directly in judgment and blessing. And in the New Testament, Paul affirms that human governments are ordained by God (Romans 13:1ff.).

To say all this is not to deny that the Bible presents real people as acting and living in real situations. It is merely to claim that the people of faith in Bible times had such a sense of the sovereignty of God that they saw his activity at all times and at all levels. This they affirmed without denying that God often acted through what we would call natural events or specific people. A good example is afforded by the personal history of Joseph. His brothers sold him as a slave and thus he was taken into Egypt, seemingly to be lost to his family. Yet what was intended as an evil action, God turned into a means of blessing to the sons of Jacob (Genesis 50:20).

Although God's universal rule is beyond understanding, aspects of it are more obvious in the history of Israel up to the time of Christ than in the history of the world since the time of Christ. The reason for this is that we have the sacred record of God's covenant relationship with Israel, and from this we can learn much of his rule in Old Testament times. In contrast, we have no equivalent key to unlock the meaning of events in modern history when God's elect people are found not in one nation, but in many nations. This is why it is difficult to give a complete answer to the question, "What is God doing in the world today?" This question is asked by many modern Christians who desire to know what is the will of God for society in general and what they should do to work for God. A tentative answer will be given later in this chapter.

Here I would like to emphasize that the arrival of the future kingdom of God in the life and ministry of Jesus Christ has had important repercussions in world history. Take, for example, the case of traffic on a busy road being held up while an injured person is being cared for and an ambulance is awaited. Or take the example of the appeal being made (as I write) through television, newspapers, etc. for the relief of suffering and starvation in Cambodia and Thailand. It is probable that the traffic would not have stopped and that no appeal would have been made had the kingdom of God not entered human history in the incarnate Son of God.

The arrival of the Christian proclamation and presence brought into human history a new idea of what being human means. The value of individual lives which

Christianity affirms has been taken up (often, regrettably, without the gospel) by human societies. Thus in
origin the whole movement for human rights, civil
rights, and the freedom of colonial or enslaved peoples
may be traced to the proclamation of the kingdom of
God.

Other examples of major repercussions may be given.
One would be marriage, sexuality, and family life which
(though it may be in decline now in the West) was origi-
nally ennobled by the impact of the Christian gospel.
Two more examples would be the desacralizing of the
State and of the powers of nature. The Christian principle that "we must obey God rather than men" eventually
had the effect of making the State and king to be mortal,
not divine; also it served to introduce, in the longer
term, the idea of toleration as a political principle. And
the harnessing of nature and natural resources for the
good of mankind has only been possible because the
Christian proclamation removed ancient ideas concerning divine forces within nature.

Yet where the kingdom of God either directly or indi-
rectly has an effect on human society, the kingdom of
Satan is not far away, seeking to change the direction
and content of what has been achieved. This, with the
further point of the sinfulness of humanity, explains
why many good and noble things and movements can so
easily become the means of proclaiming the autonomy
and selfishness of man instead of the sovereign, gracious rule of the Lord.

Returning to what is clearly affirmed in the Scriptures, we must note that a part of the presentation of
Jesus as the exalted Messiah and Lord is his rule over
the universe. After his resurrection Jesus himself said,
"All authority in heaven and on earth has been given to

me" (Matthew 28:18). John presented the Lord Jesus as the exalted Lamb of God who would certainly overcome his enemies since he is "Lord of lords and King of kings" (Revelation 17:14). And Paul spoke of Christ sitting at the right hand of God in the heavenly places, "far above all rule and authority and power and dominion, and above every name that is named, not only in this age but also in that which is to come; and he has put all things under his feet and made him the head over all things for the church . . ." (Ephesians 1:21, 22).

This rule of Christ is not to be thought of as existing alongside of, or separately from, the general providential rule of the Triune God. Rather, since the ascension of Christ the rule of the one God has been focused and particularized in Christ, the second Person of the Trinity who has taken to himself a human nature. Because of this, at the end of this age every tongue will "confess that Jesus Christ is Lord, to the glory of God the Father" (Philippians 2:11). Therefore, to speak of the rule of the exalted Lord Jesus or the rule of God or the rule of the Father over the universe is to speak of the same divine reality.

In closing this section, we need to affirm once more that the sovereign rule by God over the universe and its history is a basic Christian view which cannot be dropped without at the same time losing a major part of revealed truth. The God who created the universe is personally involved in its history, and he will bring it to his own conclusion, which is the kingdom of God. It is certainly true that the divine truth is presented in pictures which belong to ancient civilizations, but it is our duty to seek to understand them and then translate them wherever possible into modern thought-forms.

THE KINGDOM OF GOD AS THE GOAL OF MISSION

Mission is the work of the Triune Lord in which he commands his redeemed people, the church, to join (Matthew 28:19). It begins in the internal life of love of the Holy Trinity as the Father sends the Son and as the Father and the Son send the Holy Spirit into the sinful world (John 3:16; 16:7-11; etc.).Mission is that in which Jesus, the Incarnate Son, was wholly involved (Luke 4:18, 19), and it includes both proclaiming and seeing the arrival of the kingdom of God in human experience. Mission is to bring the reign of the God of grace into human lives. To live under God's reign of grace is to be made whole as the power of Satan and sin are broken. Mission today is not merely the sending of "missionaries" abroad or holding an evangelistic campaign here at home. It is the total message and activity of God's people whether they are in America, Africa, or Europe; it is acting with God in his relationship to the world.

Peter, himself deeply involved in mission, spoke of waiting "for new heavens and earth in which righteousness dwells" (2 Peter 3:13). This hope is a summary of the hope of the prophets of the old covenant (see Chapter 1). We may perhaps translate this hope into modern terms as follows: The church hopes and prays for that new order of reality which already has been revealed in Jesus Christ and which will be present in full after his second coming. It will involve perfect relationship between human beings and God; between the sexes, generations, and races; and also between humans and the new sphere in which they live.

Recognizing that only God can bring in his kingdom and overcome the kingdom of darkness and sin, the church in mission follows the Lord Jesus and lives in the power of the Spirit to proclaim the arrival of the kingdom in the here and now, and to experience the wholeness of life which is now partially manifested in anticipation of the fullness of the age to come.

Mission, which has the kingdom as its goal, will have the following four necessary parts. These, we must emphasize, should all be proceeding at one and the same time, following the example of Jesus who preached, taught, forgave sins, cast out devils, and healed the sick (see Luke 4:17ff.).

First of all, it will certainly involve bringing people to confess that Jesus is the King (= Messiah and Lord) and the only means of entry into the kingdom (John 14:6). There can be no kingdom of God in the here and now unless Jesus Christ is present by the Spirit. So, in a way which is meaningful to the hearers in their own place and culture, the story of Jesus who died and rose again to live forever must be proclaimed. Christ will be offered to the world, but offered on his own terms, not on ours. God does not approve and rarely blesses our attempts to manipulate the Good News to our own ideas of what it should be. God the Father, we may say, preaches God the Son in the power of the Holy Spirit, through his chosen messengers. Only this message is, in the long term, truly a message of salvation, liberation, and wholeness. (This duty means that preachers will not only need to know exactly what is the Good News of the Bible, but they will also need to know the best way to communicate it in a specific cultural setting.)

Secondly, calling people who confess Jesus as Lord to true repentance and conversion will not be neglected. Repentance involves a radical change of mind toward God and his world, while conversion involves a radical change in life-style. Therefore, there should be in the case of adult conversions to Christ a visible change in the character of the people involved. In a country where the dominant religion is not Christian and is, for example, Hindu, one obvious change in life-style would be attendance at the Christian church and not at the local temple. But it would go much deeper than this and would involve reassessment of life in the home and in local society.

But what about conversion in Western society where there is at least a nominal assent to Christianity? Surely here true repentance and conversion will be seen in a different life-style, a life-style which is not dominated by keeping up with the people next door, by submitting to the pressures of advertising, and by passively accepting the prevalent and dominant views of the culture. Thus, in a committed Christian home the attitude toward and use of food, technological aids, television, telephone, automobiles, vacations, education, work, and family life will reflect that the kingdom has arrived. All will be seen as belonging to the King and so is to be used in his service. So many Western Christians appear to confess Jesus as Messiah without having repented and been converted. Their daily life appears to be different only in one respect from their neighbors, and that is that they go to church on Sundays. (This duty to repent and be converted surely needs regularly to be placed before our minds; pastors and teachers will need to guide Christians into an understanding of what living a Christian life in the modern Western world really means.)

Thirdly, the mission of God's church will involve waging war against all that defiles human beings and brings them into bondage to the powers of evil in the world. Though invisible, these powers are in the employment of Satan, and they work through aspects of human society and culture.

Paul describes them vividly in Ephesians 6:10-20. In one part of the world, they may foster ignorance, sickness, poverty, and discrimination, while in another they may encourage racism, false propaganda, pan-sexualism, and the virtual worship of affluence and the powers of science and technology. Thus, in a given area and culture the churches must discern what Satan is doing to bind people in his evil service, and as they proclaim the gospel they must call upon God and work to loose people from Satan's bonds. So the churches will be necessarily involved in the tasks of education, healing, social planning, and reform. Just how they are involved will be related to the nature of the particular society in which they are witnesses to the kingdom of God. No simple blueprint is available which applies to all times and in all places. The Lord Jesus and his ministry provide the true model.

Making the words of Isaiah his own, Jesus said:

"The Spirit of the Lord is upon me,
because he has anointed me to preach good news to the poor.
He has sent me to proclaim release to the captives
and recovering of sight to the blind,
to set at liberty those who are oppressed,
to proclaim the acceptable year of the Lord" (Luke 4:18, 19).

Here proclamation and activity are combined in the name and power of the LORD. In the light of this understanding of the ministry of the Messiah and in the light of the many practical exhortations in the Letters of the New Testament, churches engaged in evangelism should automatically be involved in the positive introduction of the evidences of the presence of the kingdom of God. For example, within the local church no person or family will be allowed to be poor when others have plenty and to spare (see James 5:1ff.). Also, no racial discrimination of any kind whatsoever will be practiced, for to do so not only denies the principle of creation (namely, that we are made in God's image), but also the principle of redemption (namely, that we are one in Christ—Galatians 3:28).

Fourthly, the mission of God's church will mean praying for the people of the world and their obvious needs. They do not pray for themselves, and thus the people of God must make intercession for them. Paul urged that "supplications, prayers, intercessions, and thanksgivings be made for all men, for kings and all who are in high positions, that we may lead a quiet and peaceable life, godly and respectful in every way" (1 Timothy 2:1, 2).

THE KINGDOM OF GOD AND SOCIAL/ POLITICAL ACTION

Christians concerned for justice in the world believe that God is at work within human society in order to bring in his justice. Thus, they hold, it is the duty of the church to discern this activity of God and to join him in his work.

The Old Testament makes clear and the New Testament confirms that the LORD is the God of justice. The Hebrew noun *mishpat* occurs 389 times in the Old Testament and has three types of meaning. It is used of the character and nature of God himself: "Righteousness and *justice* are the foundation of thy throne . . ." (Psalm 89:14). It is used of that which God's character and law demands of human beings: "What does the LORD require of you but to do *justice* and to love kindness and to walk humbly with your God?" (Micah 6:8). And it is used of that which the poor, the deprived, and the downtrodden ought to enjoy and which as God's children they should have: "You shall not pervert the *justice* due to the poor in his suit" (Exodus 23:6). So justice is a rich theme in the Bible. It conveys the idea that God's actions are always right—for they proceed from holy love—and the further idea that God requires all which is right according to holy love to prevail in all human relations.

It is because of considerations such as the idea of justice that Hendrikus Berkhof wrote: "In the struggle for a genuine human existence, for deliverance of the suffering, for the elevation of the underdeveloped, for redemption of the captives, for the settlement of race and class differences, for opposition to chaos, crime, suffering, sickness and ignorance—in short, the struggle for what we call progress—an activity is taking place throughout the world to the honor of Christ. It is sometimes performed by people who know and desire it; it is more often performed by those who have no concern for it, but whose labor proves that Christ truly received—in full objectivity—all power on earth" (*Christ—the Meaning of History*, p. 173). This kind of statement challenges us to look further into the idea of the kingdom of God and righteousness/justice; it also gives us hints as to what God is doing in the world.

From the doctrine that God is the Ruler of all nations and the righteous Judge, we may affirm that he does require and expect certain standards of morality among all peoples and nations. The Lord's requirements given in the Torah for a just society in Israel have been usefully summarized as follows in *The Church and Its Social Calling* (1979), p. 73:

1. Everyone's person and property are to be secure.
2. Everyone is to receive the fruit of his labors.

3. Everyone is to be secure against slander and false accusation.

4. Everyone is to have free access to the courts and is to be afforded a fair trial.

5. Everyone is to share in the fruit of the ground.

6. Everyone, down to the humblest menial and the resident alien, is to share in the weekly rest of God's sabbath.

7. Every Israelite's dignity and right to be Yahweh's freedman and servant is to be honored and safeguarded.

8. Every Israelite's inheritance in the promised land is to be secure.

9. No woman is to be taken advantage of within her subordinate status in society.

10. No one, however disabled, impoverished or powerless, is to be oppressed or exploited.

11. No one shall be above the law, not even the king.

12. Every person's God-given place in the social organism is to be honored.

13. Punishment for wrongdoing shall not be so great that the culprit is dehumanized.

14. Concern for the welfare of other creatures is to be extended to the animal world.

These requirements may be seen as exemplifying what love for the neighbor means (Leviticus 19:18, 34). The prophets of Israel condemned wickedness, poverty, hunger, immorality, faithlessness, deceit, and perversion not only in Israel, but also in the surrounding nations (see, e.g., Isaiah 13—19 and Amos 1:3-15). Paul did likewise (Romans 1:18ff.). So, it is in accord with the will of God to call a nation (by the appropriate means and methods) to at least a basic morality which upholds honesty, integrity, fidelity, justice, and mercy. This basic morality will also include a concern to help the poor, deprived, and outcasts in a society—an emphasis found in the Law of Moses (Deuteronomy 24:14ff.), the Psalms (e.g., 146:5ff.), and the prophets (e.g., Nathan's word to David, 2 Samuel 12), as well as in the New Testament (James 1:27; Matthew 25:34ff.).

From the doctrine of the future perfect kingdom of God which will come at the end of this age, as well as from the descriptions of the Messiah's kingdom of justice (Isaiah 11), it may perhaps be deduced that what God desires and will surely implement at the end of time, he must surely want (in part at least) in the present time. Thus, if there will be perfect justice, peace, love, harmony, and righteousness in the relationships of the future kingdom of God, then God approves and supports now all moves in human society which, if only feebly, move in this direction. (I recognize that this line of reasoning is not explicitly taught in the Bible, and that deductions from what *will* be to what *ought* to be may not be valid. However, I believe it is worth considering and should not quickly be discounted.)

Apart from what is involved in the idea of the kingdom of God, there are also two other principles which confirm and strengthen the conviction that churches and/or individual Christians have a definite role of promoting justice in human society. The first of these is the basic doctrine that human beings are made in the image of God (Genesis 1:27). Whatever is the full meaning of this doctrine, it certainly includes the idea that being made and loved by God, a human being should be treated in society in a manner which recognizes his relation to God. In a word, human beings should be treated justly and not victimized, discriminated against, tortured, dehumanized, or misused. The second is the doctrine that the eternal Son of God took to himself our humanity. The fact that he did this gives an immeasurable dignity to human nature which we cannot overlook.

Therefore, it would seem to be fairly clear that God is committed to the increase of justice in human society, and that he expects those who are in his kingdom to seek to promote that justice as they are involved in mission to the world. In Western nations, this would surely involve Christians penetrating society at all levels and seeking there to introduce and foster by example and word solid virtues of faithfulness, honesty, and so on. Also, it will involve using all legitimate means available to bring the law of the land into conformity with basic moral principles. In some cases, this will involve working to change the structures of society.

To stand by and to allow the so-called secular state and society to increase is, in the long term, to say goodbye to true justice in society. The Christian church is to be nothing less than the salt of the earth (flavoring society with true virtue) and the light of the world (guiding society into a knowledge of God's will). In this task there is certainly place, when it is done wisely, for public pronouncements by church synods and leaders on a moral issue—e.g., racism, abortion, and euthanasia. Nothing, however, will ever be so influential as the example and witness of the whole Christian community living by the gospel in the world, and of individuals or groups penetrating society in daily work and practicing involvement in the political and social arenas.

There are dangers which face individual Christians and, more so, churches or Christian organizations when they become involved in politics. One such danger, though a remote one for evangelicals, is politicization in which the gospel of the kingdom becomes little more than a means of justifying a particular political philosophy. It has often been observed that some of the political activity supported by the World Council of Churches appears to be either Western liberal or Marxist philosophy in Christian dress. Likewise, some American evangelical political activity appears to be conservative and right-wing, supporting the *"status quo."*

One real problem here is that the issues of modern international politics—e.g., the role of the multinational corporation, the imposition of sanctions against a country, the nature of development, an agreement on disarmaments or on the use of atomic energy—require judgments to be made on which it appears that the Christian *qua* Christian has little or perhaps nothing to say. Regrettably, the tendency is to baptize a specific approach to these issues into the name of Christ and then call that approach *the* Christian approach. However, a danger should not cause immediate withdrawal. Aware that belonging to the kingdom has social responsibilities, Christians as a whole need to think more deeply and clearly concerning how to put them into action.

Moving on, we need to affirm that true justice cannot be promoted in isolation from the central thrust of mission, or else it will lose its foundation in the kingdom of God and seek another in one or other of the humanitarian philosophies of the day. Then it will cease to be God's justice.

To say this is not to deny that various educational, medical, and relief organizations are involved in work which God approves; nor is it to deny that Christians in mission will feel it necessary to work with and support such organizations. Human beings are made in God's image and, though sinners, still often desire what is good, right, and beautiful. So the desire to help suffering human beings is real and true, and God in his providence, as Dr. Berkhof highlighted, uses this desire and these organizations to minister to his creatures. God's justice is often accomplished by means that surprise us, especially in emergency situations created by hurricane, volcano, plague, etc. Christians will at such times gladly work with all others who want to relieve the suffering. However, in long-term aid, when an anti-Christian philosophy of life may begin to surface, then Christians may choose not to work with specific relief organizations; but surely they can only do this if they are wholly involved themselves in a similar and better work which is inspired by the love of God. For of all people, Christians have the greatest incentive to be involved in bringing justice and mercy into human society; they are servants of the Lord of justice and love, who will judge them by their actions (Matthew 25:31ff.).

CONCLUSION

This chapter has raised all kinds of difficult problems and questions. At the same time, positive themes run through it. First of all, God is the Ruler of world history and he will bring it to his own conclusion. Here is a source of confidence and security to the church and the believer. Secondly, the gospel of the kingdom is a call not only for personal trust in God and in Christ, but also a call for a radical change (repentance) in attitude and life-style. Here is a source of challenge both to the Church and the Christian family. Thirdly, preaching the kingdom to people must take into account the real situations in which they live, so that the liberation of the kingdom will be experienced in concrete ways. Here is a call for the whole gospel to be proclaimed in the full power of the Spirit by a community who live by the gospel. And fourthly, being disciples of the kingdom brings social responsibilities which must be worked out in the pursuit of justice in human society. Here is a task which needs to be done, and to be done with great preparation and care.

Here is a statement of Christian social responsibility taken from the *Lausanne Covenant* (1974):

We affirm that God is both the Creator and the Judge of all men. We therefore should share his concern for justice and reconciliation throughout human society and for the liberation of men from every kind of oppression. Because mankind is made in the image of God, every person, regardless of race, religion, color, culture, class, sex or age, has an intrinsic dignity because of which he should be respected and served, not exploited. Here too we express penitence both for our neglect and for having sometimes regarded evangelism and social concern as mutually exclusive. Although reconciliation with man is not reconciliation with God, nor is social action evangelism, nor is political liberation salvation, nevertheless we affirm that evangelism and socio-political involvement are both part of our Christian duty. For both are necessary expressions of our doctrines of God and man, our love for our neighbor and our obedience to Jesus Christ. The message of salvation implies also a message of judgment upon every form of alienation, oppression and discrimination, and we should not be afraid to denounce evil and injustice wherever they exist. When people receive Christ they are born again into his kingdom and must seek not only to exhibit but also to spread its righteousness in the midst of an unrighteous world. The salvation we claim should be transforming us in the totality of our personal and social responsibilities. Faith without works is dead.

This statement is an excellent starter for promoting

serious thinking about the kingdom of God and society, and as such I commend it to my readers.

QUESTIONS FOR DISCUSSION

1. What form of common life-style should a local church adopt in order to reflect in the world its membership in the kingdom of God? And what life-style should a Christian family adopt in order to honor Christ as King in modern conditions?

2. Since the LORD requires justice in human society, when is the church right to make a determined effort to change basic structures of society in order to remove such injustices as poverty, discrimination on class/racial/caste lines, etc.?

8 THE KINGDOM AND THE FUTURE

Speculation or inquiry into the future is common to many Westerners, as the widespread use of horoscopes shows. Among some Christians, it often takes the form of a fascination with and search for the "signs of the times"—signs for the arrival of the millennium or for the close of the age. These signs are usually of a definite political or social kind, including the progress of the State of Israel, the tension between East and West, and the decay of public morals in Western society. Popular religious paperbacks which claim to recognize and to interpret the signs often sell in great numbers today, just as books on supposed earlier signs (e.g., Napoleon's capture of Rome or the French Revolution) likewise had big sales in the eighteenth and nineteenth centuries.

I often wonder why so many Bible-based Western Christians become fascinated and even totally absorbed by the search for supposed "signs." The only reason I can supply, is that the signs, which are usually "hard facts" in today's world, act as evidences or proofs to show to sincere believers that God is really alive and at work in the world. We all know how difficult it is to believe in God in the here and now of the urban, concrete jungle. Thus, signs function as "aids" revealing, it is held and hoped, that God is in control.

The subculture of conservative Bible-believers is far removed from the explicit philosophy of many leaders of thought in the West. Yet in one particular they are often united; that is in their general, uncritical commitment to the continuing use of modern technology. Regrettably, in Western society a majority of people do not know of, or have rejected, the Christian teaching of the coming of the kingdom of God. Therefore, confidence in the future is placed not in God, but in the ingenuity of man. In particular, confidence is placed in the power of applied science, technology, and the computer, and in other means to guarantee a safe, happy, and planned future for human beings.

Some philosophers present what may be called an evolutionary futurology. A good example is the writings of the Club of Rome, an association of prominent philosophers, sociologists, economists, politicians, and scientists. They see the possibility for Western society of developing and solving its problems as it carefully plans and controls the future, relying heavily on the calculations of the computer. There is, of course, a similar confidence in technology and human ingenuity in the U.S.S.R. and among Marxists, but here it is allied to a particular philosophy of history, and so may be called a revolutionary futurology. Many ordinary people have basically the same confidence as the intellectuals, but they do not express their hope with the same clarity and coherence. Thus, from both a capitalist and Communist perspective, the human animal is now understood to be at the center of the universe and therefore at the center of hope for the future. And because death always poses problems, Western society has gone to great lengths to protect people from the reality of death. Think, for example, of the way in which funeral directors function today in contrast to a few decades ago.

The confidence of the Christian for the future is in God, and in God alone. Though he will do what is possible to improve society, his confidence will rest in God's promises to take the initiative in the future through Jesus Christ, who is the same yesterday, today, and forever (Hebrews 13:8). He believes that God's action in the future includes both judgment and mercy. At this we must now look.

THE DAY OF THE LORD

The Old Testament prophets were convinced that the civilizations which they knew would not grow or evolve into the kingdom of God. The word of the LORD which came to them caused them to teach that such was the evil within human society that judgment from God was inevitable. Therefore, they spoke of a future "Day of the LORD" when God would vindicate his own name and his righteous cause. His wrath would be poured out upon sin and evil. The picture the prophets presented was in terms of the LORD doing battle with his enemies.

Isaiah proclaimed:

For the LORD of hosts has a day
against all that is proud and lofty,
against all that is lifted up and high.

(2:12)

And,

For the LORD has a day of vengeance,

a year of recompense for the cause of Zion.

(34:8)

Jeremiah told of "the day of the Lord GOD of hosts, a day of vengeance to avenge himself on his foes" (46:10), while Ezekiel spoke of the day of the LORD being near and of it being "a time of doom for the nations" (30:3).
Joel had much to say of this great day:

For the day of the LORD is near,
and as destruction from the Almighty it comes.

(1:15)

And,

Let all the inhabitants of the land tremble,
for the day of the LORD is coming;
it is near,
a day of darkness and gloom,
a day of clouds and thick darkness.

(2:1, 2)

Amos warned the people that even for Israelites the great Day would mean judgment (5:18-20), while Obadiah warned his contemporaries that their deeds would return upon their heads in the judgment (v. 15). Zephaniah commanded the world to "be silent before the Lord GOD" as his day was at hand (1:7), and Zechariah warned of the searching nature of the judgment on this great day of the Lord (14:1).

On this day, the universal rule of the LORD will be practically and visibly demonstrated and accepted so that all the world will confess the existence and the sovereignty of the God of Abraham, Isaac, and Jacob. Of course (as was noted in Chapter 1), the prophets also spoke of the perfect kingdom of God which would follow this great day of judgment and wrath. They presented this kingdom through a variety of symbols—a restored Jerusalem, a renewed Palestine, a new heaven and earth, a new relationship between God and Israel, and a great resurrection. The kingdom was the goal of God's redemptive activity.

The New Testament writers accepted the Old Testament presentation of a great day of judgment followed by the glorious kingdom of God, but they developed these themes with reference to Jesus Christ. They held that Jesus was the vicegerent of the Father, ruling the universe and the church. When he returns to earth in power and great glory, there will occur the judgment of the nations which he will execute on behalf of the Father. Matthew reported Jesus as saying, "When the Son of Man comes in his glory, and all the angels with him, then will he sit on his glorious throne. Before him will be gathered all the nations, and he will separate them one from another as a shepherd separates the sheep from the goats . . ." (Matthew 25:31, 32). Paul told the Athenians that God commands "all men everywhere to repent because he has fixed a day on which he will judge the world in righteousness by a man whom he has appointed, and of this he has given assurance to all men by raising him from the dead" (Acts 17:30, 31). As the prophets of old had spoken of God destroying his enemies at the day of judgment, so Paul spoke of God's victory over the Lawless One, some personification of evil which will appear at the end of this age. "Then the lawless one will be revealed, and the Lord Jesus will slay him with the breath of his mouth and destroy him by his appearing and his coming" (2 Thessalonians 2:8).

Inevitably the day of judgment, for which there will be a general resurrection of the dead, will include the

division of mankind; for as Jesus said, some will come
forth to the resurrection of life and others to the resurrection of judgment (John 5:29). The final judgment
determines who shall enter the kingdom of God. Paul
explained in detail what belief in the resurrection of the
body and the life in the age to come means in 1 Corinthians 15. For Paul, there were two ages: that which ran
from creation to the judgment, and that which began at
the judgment and went forward into eternity. The first
age was, by definition, an evil age, for sin entered into it
at an early stage; but the age to come is a perfect age, for
it is the kingdom of God. The hope of the Christian is
the life of the age to come, and so Paul spoke of living in
this age as good Christians and "awaiting our blessed
hope, the appearing of the glory of our great God and
Savior Jesus Christ" (Titus 2:13). Christians are heirs "in
hope of eternal life" (Titus 3:7).

Peter also spoke enthusiastically of the Christian hope
of eternal life in the age to come: "Blessed be the God
and Father of our Lord Jesus Christ! By his great mercy
we have been born anew to a living hope through the
resurrection of Jesus Christ from the dead, and to an
inheritance which is imperishable, undefiled, and un-
fading, kept in heaven for you, who by God's power are
guarded through faith for a salvation ready to be revealed in the last time" (1 Peter 1:3-5). Here we note the
emphasis on the resurrection of Jesus as the foundation
of the hope for the Christian, and remember that this is
one of the main themes of Paul's presentation in 1 Corinthians.

For the most moving pictures of the life of the future
kingdom of God, we have to turn to the last book of the
Bible, the Revelation of St. John, and especially chapters
21 and 22. For example:

Then I saw a new heaven and a new earth; for the first heaven and the first earth had passed away, and the sea was no more. And I saw the holy city, new Jerusalem, coming down out of heaven from God, prepared as a bride adorned for her husband; and I heard a loud voice from the throne saying, "Behold, the dwelling of God is with men. He will dwell with them, and they shall be his people, and God himself will be with them; he will wipe away every tear from their eyes, and death shall be no more, neither shall there be mourning nor crying nor pain any more, for the former things have passed away."

(Revelation 21:1-4)

And later:

And I saw no temple in the city, for its temple is the Lord God the Almighty and the Lamb. And the city has no need of sun or moon to shine upon it, for the glory of God is its light, and its lamp is the Lamb. By its light shall the nations walk; and the kings of the earth shall bring their glory into it, and its gates shall never be shut by day—and there shall be no night there; they shall bring into it the glory and the honor of the nations. But nothing unclean shall enter it, nor any one who practices abomination or falsehood, but only those who are written in the Lamb's book of life.

(Revelation 21:22-27)

Having caught a vision of this hope, we must now look at its practical implications.

THE PRACTICAL VALUE OF THE HOPE OF THE KINGDOM

To possess hope in God on the basis of his Christ-centered promises is to promote God-centered rather than man-centered living. The promises of God, referring to a future supernatural reality, are of necessity presented in the language of symbol and metaphor, but this in no way detracts from their validity. Trusting in God, the Christian community and the Christian believer face the future with humble confidence. In the assurance of faith, God is known to be in ultimate control. So the believer faces the crises, tensions, claims, and arrogance of modern technological civilization, recognizing that whatever the outward appearances are, men and their computers do not ultimately rule the world. As a member of the human race, he shares with others in the agonies and exhilarations of modern life. Like Solomon, he learns that there is a time to laugh, to cry, to mourn, to heal, to listen, and to speak (Ecclesiastes 3:2ff.). Yet he differs from those with whom he lives and works in that his hope is solidly anchored to the rock of God's Word. He trusts in God and, as far as the ultimate future is concerned, in God alone.

Having such hope, both the individual and the churches should adopt a life style which reflects it. The teaching of Jesus concerning the ethics of the kingdom and the teaching of Paul concerning what it means to be a Christian in the pagan society of the Graeco-Roman world were addressed to ordinary people to show them that seeking the kingdom of God had profound implications. Some of these we examined in the chapters on ethics and society. In this area of adopting an appropriate life style for the late twentieth century, modern Christians appear to have made little progress. The fact is that it is often impossible to tell who in a given street, university, factory, or store is a Christian. Where there is active persecution of Christians, then they have to confess their faith and, in God's strength, face the consequences. Where there is a general acceptance of the Christian religion, but where the society is nevertheless basically ungodly, the adoption of a Christian life style which commends the Christian hope is urgently in need of development and implementation. Experiments to this end are to be welcomed and encouraged.

In terms of the development of justice in society, Christians who have a sure hope should be the leaders of creative thinking concerning the use of technology in human society. The power which the products of technology (e.g., computers, cars, central heating or cooling systems, television, telephones, etc.) possess in Western society is immense, and unless they are pressed into the service of justice they become the "new demons" replacing the old demons of pre-industrial society. They embody the "principalities and powers" which Paul held that we fight in Christ's name. Because Christians have a sure hope, centered on God, not man, they have the moral and spiritual resources to call for the just use of the developments of modern technology.

A PERTINENT QUESTION

Two facts raise an important question. The facts are that the Lord Jesus has not yet returned and that death, "the last enemy" (1 Corinthians 15:26), still faces us. Thus the question arises: What happens to the Christian believer at death?

It appears that Christians in the first century lived in the expectation of the second coming of Christ in their lifetimes. So the books of the New Testament reveal only a minimal interest in this question. For us, it has a greater importance since we look back over centuries of church history and the deaths of thousands of believers.

We must begin our answer by acknowledging that the prominent emphasis in the Christian hope of the New Testament is the glorious return to earth of the Lord

Jesus. Yet from various hints, occurring here and there, we are able to affirm that at death believers are not separated from the Lord to whom they have been united in the Holy Spirit. Paul declared that "whether we live or whether we die, we are the Lord's" (Romans 14:8).

Jesus told the parable of Dives and Lazarus which contains the clear implication that after death the "real person" has an existence either with or without God, in "Abraham's bosom" or "in Hades . . . in torment" (Luke 16:19ff.). And from the cross Jesus told the penitent thief, "Truly, I say to you, today you will be with me in Paradise" (Luke 23:43).

Certainly no theoretical explanation of the intermediate state is supplied in the New Testament. Those teachers who erect a doctrine of the supposed sleep of the soul from death until the resurrection do not use Scripture wisely. It is true that both Jesus and Paul referred to death as "sleep" (see Matthew 9:24; Mark 5:39; John 11:11, 13; 1 Corinthians 15:20, 51), but they were using the word in a metaphorical rather than a scientific or technical way. They were not proposing that at death the soul is separated from the body in order to go into a kind of cold storage until the great day of resurrection!

All we can say is that at death, which appears to be so destructive, the Christian will not be separated from his Lord. Paul asked, "Who shall separate us from the love of Christ?" and went on to conclude that "neither death, nor life, nor angels, nor principalities . . . will be able to separate us from the love of God in Christ Jesus our Lord" (Romans 8:35-39). He also told the Philippians, "For me to live is Christ, and to die is gain" (1:21).

Therefore, we must conclude that we cannot on the basis of scriptural evidence be dogmatic about *how* we shall be with the Lord between death and the moment we receive our glorious resurrection bodies in preparation for the life of the kingdom of God. Our certain hope is that we shall be forever with the LORD in death, through death, and on into the life of the age to come. As to the fate of the unbeliever at death and before the Last Judgment, the Scriptures have little to say and speculation will not edify.

In the medieval Catholic Church there developed a doctrine of the intermediate state which is usually called purgatory and which the Roman Catholic Church has held since Reformation times. The Orthodox Churches hold a similar doctrine. The essence of it is contained in the basic meaning of the verb "to purge," which is "to purify." The idea is that the sanctifying process which occurs on earth in the life of a believer through the work of the Holy Spirit is continued after death in preparation for the great day of resurrection. On this basis of the continuing process of purification, it is held that prayers for the dead are as valid as prayers for the living. In cases where it is held that the dead in Christ are already purified (as in the case of martyrs and saints), then their prayers for the living can be requested.

Protestants have never been happy with the doctrine of purgatory—firstly, because of the lack of biblical evidence to support it; and secondly (and probably more importantly), because of the cluster of beliefs and practices (e.g., selling indulgences) which came to surround the basic belief. Prayers for the dead, however, are sometimes offered by those who have no clear doctrine of purgatory, and they presumably work on the assumption that since we are all one in Christ, it is reasonable to pray for our brothers and sisters who have died in Christ.

Therefore, we see that the Christian hope is of such a

nature that the believer must face death trusting in the mercy of the Lord to keep him in and through death. And the church must give believers every help and confidence to do this by its humble yet confident teaching that there will be a resurrection unto life and that we should pray, "Come, Lord Jesus!" (Revelation 22:20).

QUESTIONS FOR DISCUSSION

1. Should Christians be separated because of different interpretations of the "thousand years" of Revelation 20? In terms of the total Christian hope, is the idea of a millennium only a small part?

2. What kind of Christian life style will commend the Christian hope?

FURTHER READING

POPULAR LEVEL

1. Bright, J. *The Kingdom of God*. Nashville: Abingdon, 1978. A full account of the Old Testament background.

2. Ladd, G. E. *The Gospel of the Kingdom*. Grand Rapids, Mich.: Eerdmans, 1978. A reliable presentation of the teaching of Jesus.

3. Toon, Peter. *Jesus Christ Is Lord*. Valley Forge, Pa.: Judson Press, 1979. An exposition of the kingship and kingdom of Jesus Christ.

4. Verkuyl, J. *The Message of Liberation in Our Age*. Grand Rapids, Mich: Eerdmans, 1970. An explanation of what preaching and living in the kingdom means today.

A MORE ADVANCED LEVEL

1. Berkouwer, G. C. *The Providence of God*. Grand Rapids, Mich.: Eerdmans, 1952. This includes an explanation of the sovereign rule of God over the universe.

2. *The Church and Its Social Calling—A Report*. Grand

Rapids, Mich.: Reformed Ecumenical Synod, 1979. A useful statement of the relation of kingdom, church, and society.

3. Clouse, R. G. *The Meaning of the Millennium.* Downers Grove, Ill.: InterVarsity Press, 1977. An examination of four approaches to the idea of the "millennium."

4. Kirk, J. A. *Liberation Theology.* Atlanta: John Knox Press, 1980. A critique of the understanding of the kingdom by many "liberation theologies."

5. Kraybill, D. B. *The Upside-down Kingdom.* Scottdale, Pa.: Herald Press, 1978. A Mennonite approach to the application of the ethics of the kingdom.

6. Ladd, G. E. *The Presence of the Future.* Grand Rapids, Mich.: Eerdmans, 1974. A scholarly study of the teaching of Jesus.

7. Mitton, C. L. *Your Kingdom Come.* Grand Rapids, Mich.: Eerdmans, 1978. A scholarly study of the teaching of the New Testament on the kingdom.

8. Moltmann, J. *The Church in the Power of the Spirit.* London: SCM Press, 1977. This book includes a section on the requirement of justice, freedom, etc. in human society.

9. Pannenberg, W. *Theology and the Kingdom of God.* Philadelphia: Westminster Press, 1977. A modern, sophisticated, Germanic approach.

10. Ridderbos, J. *The Coming of the Kingdom.* Nutley, N.J.: Presbyterian and Reformed Publishing Company, 1962. A thorough study of the New Testament teaching.

11. Schnackenburg, R. *God's Rule and Kingdom.* New York: Herder and Herder, 1968. An excellent biblical contribution from a Roman Catholic scholar.